PONY CARE

PONY CARE

A complete guide
to buying and caring for your first pony

Alison Pocklington

Foreword by Lucinda Green MBE

**KENILWORTH
PRESS**

First published in the UK in 2018
by Kenilworth Press, an imprint of Quiller Publishing Ltd

British Library Cataloguing-in-Publication Data
A catalogue record for this book is available from the British Library

ISBN 978 1 910016 30 5

All photographs by Shannon Daly with the exception of the photographs on pages 24 and 25 in Chapter 2 and page 179 in Chapter 13 which are credited to Nina Edminson Photography and the illustrations on pages 245 and 246 in the Glossary which are credited to Rosalia Szatanik.

Design by Arabella Ainslie

Printed in Malta

Kenilworth Press

An imprint of Quiller Publishing Ltd
Wykey House, Wykey, Shrewsbury, SY4 1JA
Tel: 01939 261616
Email: info@quillerbooks.com
Website: www.quillerpublishing.com

Contents

To my parents

For all your support, encouragement, time, patience and love.
Thank you for making my pony dreams come true.

Foreword

'The outside of a horse is good for the inside of a man.'
Winston Churchill

Never was a truer word spoken, but only if you understand your horse or pony and his needs.

As generations become further removed from the time when horses were an intrinsic and vital part of life, knowledge is no longer passed on as it once was.

Alison knows her stuff inside out and has given the benefit of such a wealth of experience and common sense a full airing in *Pony Care: A Complete Guide to Buying and Caring for Your First Pony*.

This book is a MUST HAVE for anyone who has had the tireless and repetitive call to buy from their pony-mad child. In a light and often amusing style, it outlines the many pitfalls that await in any walk of life where a horse or pony is concerned.

Packed with advice as well as cautionary tales, many will view the mountain of keeping a pony too high to scale – and for some, through circumstances, it is.

Read as a whole or dip into the glossary to brush up on specifics. This is a book to help equip all those who want to set foot in the wonderful world of horses – and stay afloat.

Lucinda Green MBE

Introduction

Most children who learn to ride dream of owning their own pony. What is often not taken into consideration is the huge difference between riding a pony once a week at the local riding school and having the responsibility of caring for a pony full time, come rain or shine.

The aim of this book is to give non-horsey parents an insight into what is actually involved in buying, owning and caring for a pony. It also offers advice on how to find the right pony, buying the necessary equipment, livery options, daily care, feeding, shoeing, health, exercise and, when the time comes, how to go about selling the pony.

Unfortunately, it is more common for people to buy the wrong pony than it is to see a child suitably matched. However, if managed well, and with good support, a difficult pony can often end up being successful. The common mistakes made when buying are usually due to lack of knowledge and experience, seeking the wrong advice and being in too much of a hurry.

Buying an unsuitable pony can very quickly have an impact on the child's confidence and interest in continuing to ride. Safety is also a very important issue. Riding and dealing with ponies will always involve a certain amount of risk, but this risk element is dramatically increased with inexperienced people.

Even the right pony can soon become a problem if managed incorrectly. This is often an unintended consequence of a lack of knowledge on how to care for the pony on a daily basis. For example, incorrect feeding can lead to bad behaviour and health issues.

Following this step-by-step guide will give you a better idea of when is the right time to buy, and how to go about purchasing and caring for the pony.

Alison Pocklington

1
Points to consider before buying

Before buying a pony it is important to consider several points. This will make it clearer if it is to be a reality or just a dream.

How long has your child been riding?

Young children are introduced into numerous sports and hobbies as they grow up. Riding tends to be introduced through a local riding school or a friend who owns a pony. Usually, children try a new hobby and stick at it if they are successful. If not, they tend to drop the activity after a few months. Buying a pony is not as straightforward as buying a

Lead rein can be fun for parents and can help your child grow in confidence.

tennis racket, once the pony has been purchased a huge amount of time and dedication is required. Therefore, I recommend that your child has willingly ridden for at least a couple of years first.

Where will the pony live?

This is one of the most important considerations. A pony cannot be kept in the garden like a dog, no matter how small he is. If you don't have land and stables at home it is important to know what the local livery options are. This will be discussed in more detail later on.

Cost of buying and keeping a pony

When considering a purchase, discuss with your adviser what they think the budget should be for the type of pony you are looking for. Do not waste time trying ponies that are far too expensive. Time wasters very quickly get a reputation for being 'joy riders'.

*Below left:
A suitable stable
yard.*

*Below right:
A well-maintained
paddock.*

MONTHLY COSTS

- Stable rent
- Bedding
- Hay and feed
- Shoeing
- Routine veterinary costs
- Dentist
- Transport
- Lessons
- Insurance.

EQUIPMENT COSTS

- Saddle
- Bridle
- Indoor and outdoor rugs (summer and winter)
- Mucking out equipment
- Feed and water buckets
- Haynet
- Grooming kit
- First aid kit
- Travel boots and tail bandage.

Parents can help out with heavy items such as haynets.

The cost of buying the pony is often not the expensive part, it is the keeping of him. It is advisable to discuss with an experienced person as to what the monthly costs will be.

Cost of equipment

Often, when buying a pony, some equipment may be included in the price or available to purchase. Other times, the pony will come with just a headcollar and rope.

Parents' knowledge on stable management

If both parents and child have no experience in looking after a pony, it is advisable to seek help and advice. It is important that the pony is fed correctly, otherwise behavioural and health issues may quickly occur. Early recognition of problems is important to avoid more serious conditions and huge vet bills.

Time involved in caring for a pony

The time involved in caring for a pony will vary depending on the livery arrangement and whether the pony is stabled or living out in the field. However, even when living out, the pony will need to be checked at least once a day. This can become time consuming when working around school and work. If the pony is stabled, much more time is required. It may not be possible to ride during the week as school and work commitments often take up too much time. Weekends and school holidays may be the only option. If this is the case, arrangements must be made to keep the pony exercised during the week. Someone must also be available to assist in the case of illness, an emergency or when going away on holiday.

Positives of buying a pony

Buying a pony can be rewarding and pleasurable for the whole family. Here are some of the positive points.

Benefits for the child

- Riding is a healthy hobby.
- Caring for and riding a pony provides your child with exercise and fresh air.
- The child will be responsible for caring for an animal, learning that the pony's welfare comes first.

- Riding can be a very social hobby. Therefore, the child will hopefully meet new people, learn to work with others and improve their social skills.

- Owning a pony is a full-time occupation and can be an ideal distraction from getting involved with the wrong crowd.

- Riding can provide goals, especially if the child eventually starts competing or working towards Pony Club tests. They will also learn valuable life skills as they deal with the ups and downs of success and failure.

Below: At unmounted Pony Club rallies, children can learn about pony care.

Far right: Owning a pony can be great for self-esteem.

'Ella benefits from owning and caring for her pony in many ways. Her relationship with her pony is very positive for her self-esteem (particularly if there is a rosette involved). She has also learned that ponies can be very frustrating and things go wrong. She falls off and gets back on — and keeps trying. I think this is a very valuable ethos for life!

The discipline of looking after her pony come rain or shine is extremely valuable. She enjoys learning about looking after her and has become a self-styled mucking out guru (at the weekend only if there is nothing better to do!). She enjoys the stable management routine and gets pleasure out of improving in the tasks — whether it's successfully picking a foot up or putting a rug on by herself.

As a very tall child Ella has benefited from riding, it has helped develop her balance and coordination. Riding helps Ella to control her emotions. She realises that getting wound up and emotional has a negative effect on Storm's behaviour and tries to control herself!

It is lovely to have a passion in common with your child. It is exciting to help them prepare for a competition and to share the ups and downs! Often whilst hacking she will relax and be more communicative about something that concerns her.

Rebeka

Caring for a pony is a fabulous adventure.

Benefits for the parents

Owning a pony can be very rewarding for parents as well:

* It enables you to spend quality time with your child. Unlike other hobbies and sports, you will be much more involved.

* It will improve your health, as you will be spending more time outdoors and getting lots of exercise.

* Parents who have never ridden will find themselves learning a new skill as they become involved in caring for the pony. It may even tempt you to take up riding yourself.

* You will meet lots of new people and possibly develop friendships.

* If your child joins Pony Club, it is expected that parents volunteer to help at rallies, camps and events. This is a great opportunity to speak to the other parents, discuss problems and seek advice. In time, you may be asked to become a committee member of the Pony Club or Riding Club.

Parents can join in with the fresh air and exercise.

'There is nothing like riding a pony for learning excellent lessons in resilience, the power of practice and understanding how important thoughts and doubts are in allowing you or hindering your success. There are always hurdles to jump with ponies and it is difficult to believe sometimes that you can get over them. But the growth that comes from finally succeeding is an amazing learning experience. There are the obvious lessons in responsibility and commitment and having to put another's needs before your own. But the other really big thing for me is there is so much fun. Fay is outside doing things, engaged in something real and we are having a fabulous adventure together. No matter how long it lasts we will have these wonderful memories forever.
Catherine *'*

A hands-on mum helps with Pony Club preparations.

Try to avoid becoming the overambitious or ultra-competitive parent. It is commonly seen in many sports, not just riding, and is one of the main reasons children quit. If you become too pushy or hard on your child, they will quickly lose confidence and interest. Try not to compare your child to others, as all children develop at a different pace. Equally, do not be tempted to rush out and buy a 'better' pony because yours is not as talented as others you see. Your child may not yet be ready for the next pony and this could set them back. Once a child becomes confident in their ability and develops a trusting relationship with their pony, progress will be made in leaps and bounds.

2

When is the right time to buy?

Choosing
the right time to buy is difficult and will very much depend on the parents' knowledge and experience or that of a friend or instructor who might be willing to help. A child who comes from a horsey background will often have had a pony bought for them at a very early age, or sometimes even before they are born! This is fine when the parents themselves have the experience of riding and looking after horses. In this situation, the horses and ponies usually live at home and the child grows up watching the parents. This does not apply for a child who has learned to ride at the local riding school once or twice a week. Here are some questions to consider and advice on gaining the necessary information and knowledge before buying a pony.

Riding lessons will help your child to improve their riding skills.

What level of rider should the child be?

When coming from a non-horsey background, I would not advise buying until the child is riding quite competently off the lead rein. This is because a young child being led around is often quite happy and confident, but that can often change when the lead rein comes off. The best place to make this transition is at a riding school in an enclosed area with a qualified instructor, not in the middle of a big field or going down the road with an inexperienced mummy or daddy. A riding school pony tends to know his job and will help the child develop the skills required to ride off the lead rein. This may not be so easily done riding a pony alone. The child needs to be confident enough that they are not relying on parents to be holding on every stride. A nervous child will often result in a nervous parent, the two combined can cause the pony to become unsettled. This could very quickly result in the child losing confidence and deciding they do not want to ride anymore. Therefore, I would advise that the child is happy to walk, trot and canter in the arena and an open space on a well-behaved pony before purchasing.

Does the child always want to ride?

Consider in the last two years how often your child has ridden. Have there been periods when he or she has 'gone off riding' and decided that they want to have a break. Are they put off in winter when it's cold and wet? Would they sometimes rather give it a miss because they are tired or their friends are doing something more exciting? If this is the case, then owning a pony is not for you and it is much better to continue riding weekly at the riding school where the twenty-four-hour and seven-day-week commitment is not necessary.

'*First pony I would definitely have on trial and for longer rather than being swept up in the excitement that the children generated. Turned out to be super but was a bit rash now I think about it as I hadn't owned anything for fifteen years!*

Riding has encouraged all three children to think about themselves and looking after another creature from the age of five will give them good independence qualities, I think!

They are also quite tough and fearless and tend not to moan too much about being wet/cold/muddy, etc. from being sent off hunting.
Nicola '

Above: This active, outdoor sport can be exhilarating and fun once the basics have been mastered.

Right: Children develop trusting relationships with their pony.

Above: A young rider will grow in confidence as they develop and improve.

Left: Enjoying an autumn morning out hunting.

25

What other hobbies does the child have?

If your child is involved in lots of other sports and hobbies it may not be the right decision to look into owning. Younger children tend to follow what they are good at. If they are particularly sporty or interested in dance or drama, you may find that you are spending a lot of money on a pony that only gets ridden twice a week due to other activities. If this is the case, it makes more sense to save money and continue to ride at the riding school.

Parents can help novice riders make tack adjustments from the ground.

School days

Consider the amount of time your child has on a school day. As they get older, the pressure of school work increases. Being able to ride after school becomes more challenging during the winter months as daylight hours are shorter, unless you are fortunate enough to have access to an indoor or floodlit arena.

Time of year

When deciding to buy a pony, the time of year should be taken into consideration. At the end of autumn, ponies can often be bought cheaper. Many people will not want to keep a pony whose rider has lost interest, or one that has been outgrown, throughout the winter months.

The cost of keeping a pony can increase during these months as it is often necessary to stable and feed. While buying can be cheaper, it has the disadvantages of costs and short, cold winter days to look after him and ride. This can very quickly put your child off. If a pony is going to misbehave it is more likely to do so when stabled more and the weather is colder.

Buying in spring and summer may mean the pony costs a little more but the new experience of becoming an owner will be much more pleasurable in better weather conditions and longer daylight hours. The start of the summer holidays is ideal as there will be plenty of time for the child to ride and get to know their new pony.

Friends with ponies

The thought of owning a pony is very exciting – in reality, it is also hard work. Children are less likely to find it a chore if they are around friends who also have ponies. The mucking out, grooming and other activities can become fun, even on a cold winter's evening. More often than not, it is when children reach their teenage years that they give up riding if they don't have friends sharing this mutual interest.

Cleaning up the yard together is great for teamwork and friendships.

Stable management

Knowledge and experience in caring for a pony is more important than the level of riding. The perfect pony can soon become a nightmare if managed incorrectly. The child who rides weekly at a riding school may often have a pony handed to them that is groomed, tacked up and ready to go. After the lesson the pony is then taken away to be dealt with. This is often the case as it is easier for the riding school to have experienced staff do the job than to supervise half a dozen children running around trying to tack up ponies.

Health and safety has a huge influence on what yards will allow clients to do with horses and ponies. Unfortunately, this system does not help your child learn and gain experience. There are numerous books and DVDs to help with learning about stable management, but putting this into practice is not so easy and should initially be done under supervision. More accidents occur on the stable yard than in the arena; even the smallest pony is capable of causing severe injuries to a child or adult if care is not taken.

Children having a pony care demonstration.

It is therefore essential that both child and parents gain some experience before buying. This can be done in a number of ways. Some riding schools may offer 'pony days' or even 'pony camp'. This is where the child is given the opportunity to spend the day with a pony and, along with riding lessons, they will carry out all the tasks required to care for a pony on a daily basis. It may also include some formal lectures on feeding, shoeing and health issues. If the riding school does not offer this in a group situation, it is worth asking if something can be booked in privately.

Some equine colleges or British Horse Society (BHS) training yards may offer stable management courses. These are more suited to adults and teenagers. Contact the local Pony Club or Riding Club to see if they have any pony days or training days. They may also be able to put you in contact with a freelance instructor who could offer some training.

Tell your riding instructor that you are considering buying a pony and ask if it would be possible to spend some time at the stables, watching and helping. This used to be very common and one of the best ways of gaining experience. Unfortunately, due to health and safety regulations, many establishments are now wary of doing this because of the amount of supervision required.

Having a friend who already has a pony is ideal. Spending time watching and helping is lots of fun and educational. It is also advisable for the parents to be involved.

Another option is to look for a yard that offers full livery. The pony will be cared for by experienced staff that are usually happy for you to be involved. This is a

Areas to cover before buying

STABLE MANAGEMENT

- **Basic handling**
- **Mucking out**
- **Grooming**
- **Feeding**
- **Turning out and catching from the field**
- **Applying rugs**
- **Tacking up**
- **Tack cleaning.**

RIDING

- **Confidently walk, trot and canter**
- **Ride in an open space**
- **Riding and road safety.**

great way to learn and get supervised hands-on experience until you are confident to look after the pony by yourself.

Catching a pony competently.

3
Finding the right pony

Finding a pony is the easy bit as there are hundreds of ponies on the market. Finding the right one is not so straightforward, even for the most experienced person. There are many honest people in the horse world who want to do their best for the pony and the potential buyer. Unfortunately, there are just as many who are not so considerate and will do anything to either make money or get rid of a problem. When purchasing for the first time, it is essential that you are aware of why things go wrong and how to go about eliminating risks.

Why the wrong pony is purchased

Overkeen first-time buyers will often go ahead without seeking any advice. Buyers may find a pony through an advert or sale and buy it

Pony Val with her devoted young owner.

without having asked the right questions or getting the opinion of a qualified or experienced instructor. Dishonest sellers will quickly pick up on naive, inexperienced buyers and can often take advantage.

Seeking the right advice

Care must be taken when asking for help in finding a pony. It is essential that the adviser knows your child's ability and confidence level. It is also important that they know what your aspirations are, otherwise you may end up with a pony that has cost you more than is necessary. Also, be aware of people that offer to find you a pony and are only interested in making a commission on a sale. It is common practice that a seller will give 10 per cent of the sale price to the person who has found the client. This often leads to people being more concerned about getting their commission than finding a suitable match. Deal only with a professional that you know well and trust, such as your own instructor.

'*One of the most important first steps I found is, as we know, finding the **right** genuine first pony. The pony that will make or break the start of a riding passion.*

One of the hardest and most frustrating things that stands out for me is how many dishonest people are out there nowadays, selling unsuitable first time ponies.

It's very hard for non-horsey parents to see through this. They think they are getting a pony that does what the seller says but that is not always the case. It is also not always the way that the more you pay for the pony means the better it is.'

Georgie

A knowledgeable instructor giving a lesson.

'What would I have done differently on buying our first pony again? I would have taken someone more experienced with me right from the start or even possibly employed someone to help, then they might have been more willing to come and look with us and not let us down at the last minute, as happened with us. So we just went on our own.

We thought we had found the perfect pony, three weeks of negotiations, trialling in different environments, meeting the family, vetting them, being vetted ourselves ... it all went horribly wrong within the first twenty-four hours, and we soon realised that we had bought completely the wrong pony, we'd over-ponied Madison. She lost control and couldn't stop her. Thankfully, even though she came off, she wasn't majorly injured, apart from a few bruises and her pride taking a bashing. She was embarrassed and she took a massive knock in her confidence, but our inexperience proved the major cause here. It's a complete minefield, especially if you have no experience.

This family were lovely and we just got it wrong but they took her back with no quibbles and we parted company. It could have been so different though and we could have ended up with a new pony that was unsuitable!

Amanda

Pony Peggy moves forward while her rider listens to instructions.

Pressure to buy

Do not be rushed into making a decision because the current owner puts pressure on you. It is advisable to try the pony at least twice. The seller may say that this is not possible as they have other people wanting to try the pony. This may be a method of pressurising you into buying. The exception to this is that the pony is well sought after. This is rarely the case as such ponies are not usually advertised as they have a number of homes waiting for them.

Pressure can also come from fellow pony owners telling you how much their child has improved since owning their own pony. Your child may also nag you because all their friends have ponies.

Fed up with trying

Trying ponies can be both time consuming and frustrating. Sometimes it can take months before something suitable is found and this may then fall through due to failing the vetting. This commonly leads to people settling for something unsuitable as they think the right one will never come along.

Overambitious parents

Inexperienced parents can often be to blame. They may think that their child is more capable than they are. The parent might actually want the pony more than the child does. More often than not, this is caused by competition with other parents to have the best pony.

Looks not suitability

A common mistake is buying a pony for his looks. This could be because your child decides he wants a certain breed or colour. The ideal first pony is often not stunning to look at but has a sane temperament and a heart of gold.

Above: Small child on a large pony.

Below: Suitably sized ponies.

Criteria of a good first pony

Suitable size

A common mistake is to go for a pony that your child will grow into and that will therefore last longer. This may work for a confident child who has had experience and is moving on to the second pony, but not always for the first pony. It is better that the pony is on the small side so that the child feels safe and not intimidated. Ponies are extremely clever and very quickly pick up on a child's nervousness, often resulting in bad behaviour. Your child may look a little big on the pony, but it is rare that they will be too heavy and so it shouldn't stop them from doing the job.

Traditionally, horses and ponies are measured in 'hands'. This originates back to when the width of a person's hand was used as a measure. One hand is equal to four inches. The measurement used is referred to as 'hands high' (hh). For example:

- 13hh

- 13.1hh

- 13.2hh

- 13.3hh

- 14hh.

Ponies are also measured in centimetres. As either measurement system may be used in pony advertisements, it is important to know the correct conversion when looking for a pony.

Measurement conversion			
Hands (hh)	Centimetres (cm)	Hands (hh)	Centimetres (cm)
10	102	12.2	127
10.1	104	12.3	130
10.2	107	13	132
10.3	109	13.1	135
11	112	13.2	137
11.1	114	13.3	140
11.2	117	14	142
11.3	119	14.1	145
12	122	14.2	147
12.1	124		

The measurement is taken from the ground to the highest point on the withers, with the pony standing square on level ground with his head and neck in a natural position. The most accurate method is to use a horse measuring stick.

Many breed societies or affiliated organisations will require a pony to have an up-to-date height certificate obtained through the Joint Measurement Board (JMB). Ponies are measured annually from four to seven years old. After that, they are given a 'Full Measurement'.

Good temperament

A pony being measured on a level surface.

As mentioned before, the temperament of the pony is far more important than its looks. The pony should be kind and friendly. Children get as much pleasure from taking care of their pony as they do riding him. This is only possible if the pony is happy to be handled and groomed. It is

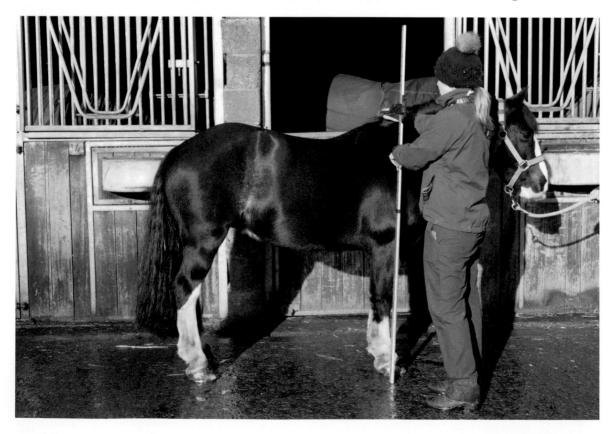

not much fun avoiding being bitten or kicked and the child's safety becomes a worry for the parents.

When ridden, the pony should be willing without being too forward going. If given the choice, it is better to choose a slightly lazy pony than one that is very sharp.

Types and breeds

Ponies come in many shapes and sizes, ranging from sturdy cobs to native breeds and to the finer Arab and Thoroughbred types. When buying your first pony, temperament is so much more important than looks. If your child has been learning to ride at the local riding school they are likely to have fallen in love with a certain pony and will want to find one very similar. It is a mistake to set out looking for a certain colour or breed, unless you are intending to compete in specific showing classes.

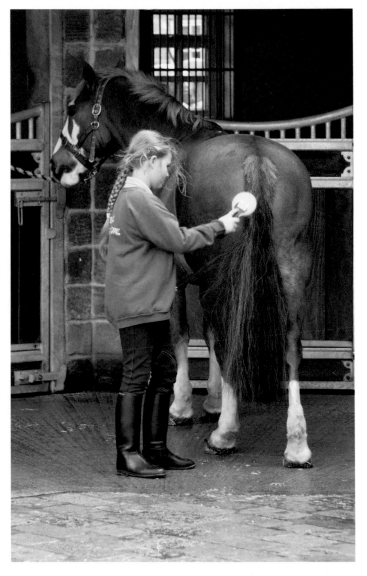

Grooming is an important part of taking care of your pony.

As a rule, cob types and native breeds tend to have a steady, calm and kind temperament. Finer bred ponies can be much sharper and more forward going, making them more suitable for higher level competition. As they get older and are ready to semi-retire, they can sometimes make excellent schoolmasters for children to learn on.

Some of the most common breeds used as children's ponies are described overleaf.

Shetland

◊ Height: up to 12.2hh.
◊ Colour: black, bay, brown, chestnut, grey, coloured.
◊ Characteristics: sturdy, short legged, cute rather than pretty, has the look of a Thelwell pony, a good weight carrier.
◊ Temperament: can be headstrong and independent.

The Shetland pony is often sought after as a first pony for a very young child. Originating from the Shetland Isles, they are tough, do well on very little food and can happily live out all year round.

Two Shetland ponies.

Welsh pony and cob

Welsh ponies and cobs are a closely related breed of native ponies originating from Wales. They are now classed into four sections by the breed society.

Section A

◊ Height: up to 12hh.
◊ Colour: any except piebald and skewbald.

◊ Characteristics: a neat compact pony with a small, attractive head, hardy and strong. A good mover and jumper.
◊ Temperament: kind, brave, intelligent, sometimes a little stubborn.

Welsh section A.

Section B

◊ Height: up to 13.2hh.
◊ Colour: any except piebald and skewbald.
◊ Characteristics and temperament: those of the Welsh section A.

Section C

◊ Height: up to 13.2hh.
◊ Colour: any except piebald and skewbald.
◊ Characteristics: a stronger version of the section B due to some cob breeding. They are sure footed and hardy, making them suitable for small adults as well as children. They are good jumpers and also used for driving.
◊ Temperament: intelligent, kind, brave.

Section D (Welsh cob)

◊ Height: over 13.2hh (no upper limit).
◊ Colour: any except piebald and skewbald.
◊ Characteristics: an attractive pony that oozes quality. Strong and powerful, they have had a lot of success in the international driving world. They also make good hunters and jumpers.
◊ Temperament: willing, intelligent, kind, brave.

Connemara

◊ Height: 12.2hh to 14.2hh.
◊ Colour: usually grey but can be bay, black, brown, dun, roan, chestnut or palomino.
◊ Characteristics: a neat, compact pony that is tough and strong. A good mover and jumper.
◊ Temperament: kind, intelligent, sensible, a popular child's pony.

Connemara.

Exmoor

◊ Height: up to 12.3hh.
◊ Colour: brown, bay, dun with black points, no white markings.
◊ Characteristics: originating from Exmoor, these ponies are tough, strong and well put together. They are good movers with lots of stamina.
◊ Temperament: alert, intelligent and kind, making them a good choice for a child or small adult.

Exmoor.

New Forest

◊ Height: 12hh to 14.2hh.
◊ Colour: any except piebald or skewbald.
◊ Characteristics: workmanlike with strong conformation and a longer, finer head than some other native breeds. They are also good movers and jumpers.
◊ Temperament: gentle, intelligent and versatile, making them an ideal riding pony.

Dartmoor

◊ Height: up to 12.2hh.
◊ Colour: any except piebald and skewbald.
◊ Characteristics: small head, sturdy body, strong with lots of stamina. They jump quite well.
◊ Temperament: reliable, sensible, quiet and kind, making them a good all round child's pony.

Dales

◊ Height: 14 to 14.2hh.
◊ Colour: mostly black, bay or brown but can be grey or roan. They may have white markings such as a star or snip.
◊ Characteristics: strong and sturdy with good, straight movement, plenty of stamina, a thick mane and tail and well-feathered legs.
◊ Temperament: intelligent, brave, sensible, kind and hardworking. They are often used as trekking ponies or for general riding, and are ideal for adults and children.

Dales.

Conformation

The conformation of the pony is important as this can have an impact on how easy he is to ride and, often, how sound he stays. Judging how well a pony is put together is not easy and requires a trained eye. Your instructor or adviser should be able to assess the pony before seeing him ridden. First, they will be looking to see how well-proportioned he is. Even an untrained eye can usually recognise that the pony's head looks far too big or that his back is very long. Next, they will look at different areas in more detail. Important factors include how correctly his neck fits onto his withers, as this affects how the pony carries his head and neck. A child will often feel unsafe if the neck is set on very low or if the pony carries his head extremely high. The back should not be too long as this can often make the pony harder to ride. The legs should be set on straight and the front and hind feet should each be a pair. This will give the pony a much stronger chance of staying sound.

Unless you are intending to show the pony, it is not necessary to look for perfection and looks are certainly not the most important aspect. When meeting a pony for the first time, remember the saying, 'handsome is as handsome does'.

Age

Avoid buying a young, uneducated pony. The first pony is there to give your child confidence and bring them on, as the child will not be experienced enough to school the pony. A pony has usually had a good, all-round education by the time he is eight, and it

'*I bought a very lovely five-year-old pony with lots of potential – but very green and flighty. Ella coped fine on the lead rein but really struggled to gain confidence off the lead rein as the pony needed reassurance and confident, clear riding. If I was to do it again, I would buy or ideally loan an old hand pony club schoolmaster who could show her the ropes without worrying about the pony's development.*'
Rebekah

An experienced pony.

would be a mistake to buy younger than this. Ponies continue well into their late teens and often early twenties, therefore do not be put off by one that is much older as he will still do the job.

Experience

Look for a pony that has done as many different activities as possible. It is good to know that the pony is happy to work alone and also does not get too excited in company. Finding a pony that has participated in Pony Club activities and hunted is ideal.

Bombproof/traffic proof

Teach your child to observe safe road procedures whilst hacking out.

Most children will want to hack out, as well as ride in the arena. If this is to be safe and pleasurable, it is essential that the pony is good in all traffic and not spooky.

Good to shoe, box and clip

These three things will make life easier for you and others that have to deal with the pony.

Vices

When possible, try to avoid buying a pony that has a vice. A vice, otherwise referred to as a stereotypical behaviour, is a bad habit that more commonly develops in stable kept horses and ponies rather than those that live out. Once developed the animal may continue the behaviour when in the field. They are thought to be caused by boredom, hunger, lack of exercise and stress. It is also believed by some that a vice can develop by one horse observing and copying another, but there is no solid evidence to back this up.

It is important to ask if the pony is vice free as a seller is not obligated to tell you if the question is not raised. Some vices are more detrimental than others.

The following sections outline the most common vices and how they may affect the pony's behaviour and health.

Cribbing or windsucking

Cribbing is when the horse or pony grabs hold of a surface, such as the top of the stable door, with his teeth and sucks in air, arching his neck as he does so. Windsucking is similar but the horse does not actually grab onto anything as he sucks in air.

Cribbing is more commonly seen in horses that spend more time in the stable than out in the field. It is thought to be caused by boredom and stress. If done excessively, it can cause damage to the teeth and stomach. The muscle on the underside of the neck can also become overdeveloped, making it difficult for the horse to work in a correct outline. An anti-cribbing collar can be worn to help prevent the horse sucking in air.

Wood chewing

This can look similar to cribbing but the pony bites the wood and does not suck in air. It is usually caused by hunger or boredom when stabled, although, once established as a habit, some ponies will chew gates and fencing in the field.

Box walking

Box walking is when the pony literally spends his time walking around the stable, usually in a small circle. In extreme cases it can be seen in the field. It is usually associated with stress. Typically, the pony is relaxed when the yard is quiet, but as soon as things get busier he becomes worried and the walking starts. This can often be separation anxiety or anticipation of exercise. It is very difficult to keep the bed clean, tidy and in place. Rubber mats used in the stable are advisable to prevent slipping. The pony may lose condition and it can sometimes put stress on the limbs, resulting in lameness.

Anti-weaving grill.

Weaving

Weaving is when the pony rocks from side to side, transferring his weight from one foreleg to the other. Like box walking, it tends to be stimulated by activity on the yard. It is mostly seen in the stable but can occur in the field. Ponies tend to be more prone to weaving when looking out over the stable door, and will often stop when the top door is closed. It can lead to weight loss and lameness due to the stress on the limbs. Anti-weaving grills can be fitted to stable doors to help prevent it, but they do not cure the vice.

Biting and kicking

Ponies are not usually born with an aggressive temperament but may develop one through bad experiences, which can lead to pain, loss of trust or irritation. This is often caused by lack of knowledge, poor management and bad handling. A pony will usually give warning signs before biting and kicking such as laying his ears back, swishing his tail and grinding his teeth. If these cautionary behaviours are ignored or he is treated aggressively, he may feel threatened and become more defensive, leading to biting and kicking.

Once this has developed it takes experienced management and handling for him to regain trust. It is advisable to have a basic understanding of horse psychology and body language to work well with your pony.

A pony with their ears back may be bad-tempered.

One thing we all love to do is to give our pony treats. Unfortunately, this may encourage the pony to nibble or bite when being handled as he is looking for a tidbit. If the pony has this habit, avoid over treating and carrying them in your pocket. It is best to put the treat in a bucket or on the ground.

Where to look

Word of mouth

The best ponies tend to come by word of mouth. A good pony will usually have his next home waiting for him as someone will have seen him at Pony Club or a competition and asked the owner to contact them

'I do think going through horsey friends, word of mouth, pony club, etc. is the best way to find a pony, it's so much better if you know the pony or the people because they're more inclined to be totally honest with you. However, this can prove difficult because when you're first starting out in this field you often have no contacts whatsoever and that's really difficult.'

Amanda

when the pony is outgrown. Attend local shows or Pony Club activities to make contacts and ask if there are any first ponies coming up for sale in the near future. It is worth waiting a few months for a pony that comes with a good reputation. It may be possible to try the pony and pay a deposit to ensure he comes your way when the owner is ready to sell.

Pony Club/Riding Club

Most Pony Clubs and Riding Clubs have a website where ponies can be advertised. Finding a pony this way is ideal as he will be well known for the right or wrong reasons. It will be much easier to find out, truthfully, the pony's history and possibly trace back to a number of homes. If a pony is sourced this way, it is also worth talking to the instructors who have had him in their lessons to find out their opinion.

Pony Club.

Social media

It is very common to come across horses and ponies advertised on social media. This is often accompanied by photos and videos. The advantage of this is that people will comment on the pony, hopefully in a positive manner. When following up these adverts, it is advisable to try to find out about the seller's reputation.

Websites

There are several websites set up for advertising horses and ponies. This is very much replacing the traditional way of advertising in magazines or the local newspaper. The advantage of websites is that more photos and videos can be shown. Many ponies are sourced this way. The downside of this is that, more often than not, you are dealing with a total stranger, which can be more of a risk unless you find out the person comes with a good reputation. The seller may also be located hours away, therefore much more time and money is involved in the trying process, especially if paying a professional to look with you.

When travelling a distance, find a number of ponies in the same area to try on the day. Lots of time can be wasted travelling up and down the country. Some people prefer to have a limit on the distance they are prepared to go. This is advisable unless the pony has come to you by word of mouth with an excellent reputation.

Dealers

Dealers often come with a bad reputation, but not all are bad. However, this would not be a chosen source of seller for a first pony. The reason is that, a good pony would be sold by word of mouth and not end up on a dealer's yard.

Young ponies will often be sold through dealers' yards. An older pony, on the other hand, has probably ended up in the hands of a dealer because he has a problem and proved impossible to sell privately.

Sales

As with dealers, sales should be avoided when buying the first pony. Many top horses in racing and competition are sold through good auctions. The smaller sales up and down the country tend to accommodate horses and ponies that cannot be sold privately due to either soundness or temperament issues. Trial facilities are limited, if any, and therefore it is a huge gamble on what you are purchasing. This often means that the pony will sell for very little money, which tends to be the attraction for people with a limited budget.

'We had a few ponies on loan before we bought our first pony. Although unintentional, this worked out really well for us as it gave us time to find out what my child really required in a pony to allow her to learn and progress.

Before we embarked on this adventure I hadn't realised how different ponies' personalities are and how important it is to find a fit that will give a child a happy balance between confidence and challenge.

Catherine

Loan/lease

Loaning or leasing a pony is an option to consider before buying. A loan is an arrangement where there is not a rent as such for the pony, but the running costs must be covered. A lease will entail paying a fee for the use of the pony as well as taking on all of the daily expenses. A lease is more common for competition horses and ponies. Ponies may be offered for loan because the owner is very attached and does not want or need to sell. One child may have outgrown the pony and it is going to be a year or two before the next child is ready. Soundness issues may prevent a pony being sold but the lameness can often be managed for the level of work a first pony is required to do.

The obvious advantage of loaning is that it eliminates the initial cost of buying. However, the running costs are generally the same unless the owner agrees to continue to pay some of the expenses. This is not usually the case unless it is a part loan or share agreement. The other advantage is not having the trouble of selling the pony if the child loses interest or when it is outgrown.

If considering a loan, it is essential that a legal loan agreement is put in place and signed by both parties. It is essential to include each party's costs and responsibilities, agreement on insurance, veterinary fees and unexpected termination of the loan. The BHS website provides a sample loan agreement.

Part loan

It may be possible to find a pony to part loan. This involves sharing the pony with the owner, usually for financial reasons or lack of time. More often than not, the owner will request that the pony remains at his current home and you take on some of the responsibilities of his care and contribute financially. They will then state what you are allowed to do with him. For example, you may be given certain days of the week that he is, in effect, your pony and you are free to do whatever activities

Children sharing a pony.

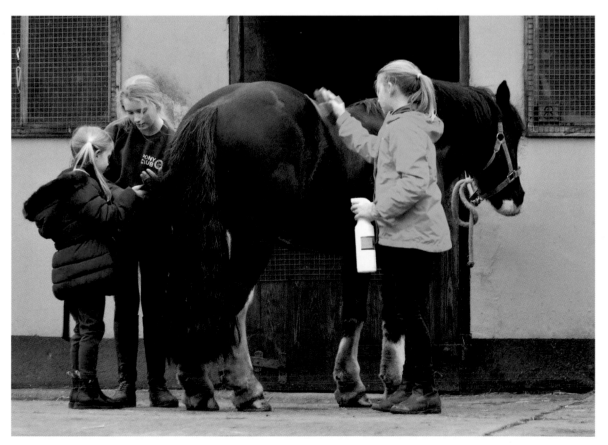

you like. Other arrangements may state that you are only allowed to ride the pony at home or on hacks; in other words, you are simply assisting in keeping him exercised.

Both arrangements do have the advantage of introducing your family to what is involved in owning a pony without spending too much money and totally committing to it.

The disadvantage is the owner will probably take priority on what the pony does, which may leave you fairly limited. This could work well in the beginning, but if your child is keen it is inevitable that they will soon be wanting more.

If a part loan came along, it could be viewed as a stepping stone: although your child may want more, it is an ideal way to test how dedicated they really are and if buying is the right decision.

4

Trying the pony

When making an inquiry about a pony, it is essential to have a list of questions to ask over the phone. Have the questions written down and a pen and paper ready to take notes.

QUESTIONS TO ASK THE SELLER

◊ Asking price

◊ Description – height/breed/age/gender

◊ Why is the pony for sale?

◊ How long have they had the pony?

◊ How old and what level was their child when they bought the pony?

◊ What activities have they done with him?

◊ What activities had he done with previous owners?

◊ Contact details of previous owners

◊ What is his temperament ridden and in the stable?

◊ Is he sociable with other ponies/people?

◊ Is he good to

» lead

» groom

» tack up

» catch

» shoe

» clip

» load and travel?

◊ Is he bombproof and traffic proof?

◊ How does he behave in an open space?

◊ Does the pony live in or out?

◊ How does he behave if other ponies leave him?

◊ Any vices?

◊ Any health issues (e.g. laminitis, sweet itch)?

◊ Vaccinations?

◊ Is he easy to maintain a healthy weight?

◊ How is he when he hasn't been ridden for a period of time?

◊ What clubs are they in (e.g. Pony Club, Riding Club)?

◊ Name and contact details of their main instructor

◊ Can they send photos and videos of the pony performing?

◊ What tack is the pony ridden in?

The next step is to arrange a time to see and try the pony. This can often be difficult to arrange during school term time. However, it is not advisable to wait too long as a good pony will sell quickly and the seller will not want to hang around and miss a sale. They may also not be in a position to look for their next pony until the current one is sold.

Facilities

Always ask what facilities are available to try the pony. Take into consideration that your child is likely to be nervous getting on a strange pony in a new environment. A big open field may not be the best place, especially if it is wet and windy. If the present owner can only offer this, ask if there is a local yard with an arena available that you can hire. It may be an advantage to try the pony away from his home.

A suitable arena for trying a pony.

Trying

Always give yourself plenty of time to view and try the pony. Remember, this is the start of an exciting journey for your child and it should be enjoyable and stress free.

It is advisable to take a more experienced person along with you, ideally your child's instructor. It is also useful to see a more experienced child ride the pony. This could be an older sibling or friend.

Below left: A friendly pony.

Below right: A not-so-friendly pony.

When meeting the pony for the first time, take note of certain points. Usually the pony will be in the stable, clean and presentable for the occasion. Note how the pony greets the owner, does he look happy to see them or does he put his ears back and turn away? It would be preferable to see the pony being dealt with by his present rider rather than an adult. This would indicate that the child enjoys spending time with him and is confident doing so.

Cast an eye around the stable to look for signs of stable vices. Chewed wood or kick marks are not a good sign. If the door has an anti-weaving grill, ask if that has been put there specifically for this pony.

Alarm bells should ring if, on arrival, the pony is already tacked up or has sweat marks showing he has already been worked that day. First, introduce yourself to the pony in the stable. It is likely you will have seen photos and videos of the pony. Does the pony in front of you resemble the one in the photos?

Next, ask for any rugs to be removed and for him to be brought out of the stable in a headcollar. If the owner prefers to use a bridle this could be an indication that the pony is not well mannered in hand. Ponies often learn they can easily get away from a small child or adult when wearing only a headcollar. This is not the end of the world, but training will be needed to rectify this. Have a general look over the pony.

An experienced person assessing conformation.

View the pony being led at the walk and at a trot.

A more experienced person should look closely at the pony's conformation and feel down the legs for blemishes. They may ask if it is okay to look in the mouth to age the pony and check for problems with the teeth. This is also a good time to look at the passport.

The pony should then be examined in hand. This involves the pony being walked away and towards you, and then the process repeated in trot. Your adviser can then check to see if the pony is sound (not lame) and how he moves. If you are happy so far, the pony can then be tacked up. If it is not love at first sight, don't be too hasty about not continuing. Maybe the pony is not as handsome as you had hoped but, as mentioned previously, temperament is more important than looks. On the other hand, if the pony has shown signs of being aggressive, difficult or lame in this first assessment, it may not be worth continuing and wasting everyone's time.

If possible, ask if your child can help tack up the pony. It is more desirable to see this being done by a child. Another cause for alarm bells is if there is not a child present to show the pony. Under no circumstances should you put your child on without first having seen someone else ride the pony. If the child showing the pony is quite a bit older and more competent than your child, this must also be taken into consideration before your child climbs on board. At this stage, if the pony looks difficult or strong it is not suitable as a first pony.

Signs of being aggressive

- **Laying the ears back**
- **Grinding the teeth**
- **Threatening to or actually biting**
- **Tail swishing**
- **Stamping a foreleg**
- **Turning the hindquarters towards you**
- **Kicking out with the hind legs.**

A child tacking up.

Take note of what tack is being used, especially the type of bit and noseband he is wearing. Ideally, he should be in a simple snaffle and a cavesson noseband (see Chapter 12). This indicates that he hopefully has a good mouth and doesn't get strong. If this is not the case and the pony is wearing something stronger, then ask the reason for this. In some cases, it may be that this particular bit has become 'fashionable' and it was at the request of his rider for a look rather than the pony needing it. It is worth the instructor checking to see if the pony has a sore mouth, which would indicate that he can get strong. Ponies are also often put in a martingale when it isn't necessary. The purpose of a martingale is to prevent the pony getting his head above the point of control. The first pony should not show this trait. Therefore, the martingale should not be necessary and you should request to see the pony ridden without it. The pony should wear a neck strap. It is also worth a discreet check of the girth straps, stirrup leathers and reins to check the stitching looks safe.

A neck strap can be used to give your child something extra to hold onto whilst they are learning to ride, so they don't pull on the pony's mouth.

The pony should be shown in walk, trot and canter. A few show jumps should be made available if you are intending to use the pony for jumping at some stage. If you are happy with how the pony goes, then your child can ride. However, if at this stage for some reason it is clearly not the pony for you, it is better to halt proceedings. The most obvious reason for this would be that he looks to be too much pony for your child, especially if he has been ridden by an older child and still looks a handful.

A tall child on a small pony.

Time should be taken to get your child comfortable with their stirrups suitably adjusted. If possible, your instructor should step in at this stage as they will feel more confident with someone they know and trust close by. The pony may feel very different to the one they have been riding and this can be quite intimidating. The child should not be pushed to get on with it, but allowed to adjust in their own time.

At this time it can be quite tempting for parents to interfere. Allow the instructor and the pony's current owner to take the lead on how best to proceed. Videoing is a useful job for the parents to do. The pony should be tried in walk, trot and canter. If the child is capable, they can pop over some small jumps. If this all goes to plan then you should request to ride the pony out of the arena in a more open space. This can be followed by a hack down the road accompanied by an adult on foot who is close at hand to step in if there are any problems. If you are at all worried by this, it is advisable to see his present rider demonstrate this first.

It will be very obvious at this stage as to how your child is feeling about the pony: if the experience has been terrifying, they will be very keen to get off; if they have loved it, then it may be difficult to persuade them to dismount.

It doesn't take long for your child to fall in love with their pony!

Allow your child to help untack and assist with washing off or grooming. It is better that the adults chat with the owner and the children deal with the pony. This is a good time to ask any more questions that have come to mind. It may be a chance to look at more photos or video of the pony

performing. It will be very obvious how fond of the pony the present owner is by the way they talk about and deal with him. If he has done a lot for their child, they will tell you how wonderful he is, giving lots of examples of his achievements. His present rider may also be sad at the prospect of having to say goodbye to a dear friend. An owner who thinks highly of their pony will ask you lots of questions regarding the pony's care and future if he comes your way. The more prepared you are for the arrival of your first pony, the more confident the present owner will be that you are a suitable buyer. If none of this occurs, it is a sign that they don't care too much about the pony and a sale is more important than his future home.

If at this stage you are very interested in the pony, then there should be a discussion regarding the next step. This should definitely involve trying the pony again. A time can be fixed up, there and then, to show the owner you are seriously interested. You may ask if it is possible to see the pony at a different venue to get more of an idea of how he behaves away from home. It may be that a discussion is needed between the instructor, child and yourself before deciding if you wish to proceed to the next stage. If this is the case, thank the owner for their time and say you will call them when you have had time to discuss. This does leave a slight risk of someone getting in there before you.

When the pony is tried for the second time, your child should feel much more confident. It would be nice to see them start where they left off and progress a little further. Most important is that the enthusiasm to ride the pony again is coming from the child and not the parent. After trying a second time, a decision often needs to be made as the current owner may have other people waiting to see the pony. This is usually discussed and slept on, giving the owner an answer the next day.

Trials

Having a pony on trial means that you are given a period of time to take the pony home, usually for a week or two to see if he is truly suitable. Many owners are reluctant to do this as there is a risk that the pony may sustain an injury or the future owner may not do the pony justice, causing a straightforward pony to return with a problem. This is more common with inexperienced first-time buyers. Due to this, it is quite rare that a trial period will be offered.

If the trial is allowed, a contract must be drawn up between the two parties stating the conditions. It is likely that the owner will request a deposit and ask that you insure the pony for the trial period.

5
Buying the pony

Once a decision has been made to go ahead and buy a pony, it is important to speed up the process as much as possible as the current owner will not be keen to wait for weeks while you organise a vetting and payment.

Value

Child excited about her new pony.

The pony should not be too expensive, as it is not expected to be a world-beater. On the other hand, safe and well-mannered ponies are hard to come across. The age of the pony will have an impact on its value. The more expensive child's pony is usually eight to fifteen years

old. As discussed previously, it is not wise to buy younger than eight years and buying an older pony may save you some money.

If the pony has health or soundness issues and will not pass a vet check, the value will be decreased. Again, for the level of work it is expected to do, this can often be managed with good advice.

The owner will have given you an asking price for the pony in your initial inquiry. Make sure you have made a note of this, as some owners may try to up the price when they see how keen you are to buy. Others may try to pull a fast one and tell you they have had more money offered by someone else. Do not be fooled by this and stick to the original price they told you or walk away, as it is likely they are not very honest people.

Making an offer

If the owner has no doubts that the pony will sell easily, they are likely to be rigid about the asking price. Sometimes a pony is advertised for £3500 o.n.o. (or nearest offer). This means that the owner is open to some negotiation and will take slightly less. Other times, the advert may say £3000 but open to offers, as a good home is more important. Again, you are likely to get him cheaper if the owner wants you to have him. Typically, £500 less than the asking price is offered and the owner meets the buyer halfway; for example, a pony advertised at £3500 may be purchased for £3250.

Tack and equipment

The advert may state that the price includes some equipment. This is often the case when the equipment is too small for the seller's next pony. If anything, it's usually the bridle and rugs that are included in the price. The saddle may be offered to you at an extra cost. If this is the case and you are interested in purchasing the saddle, have your adviser check the fit, condition and its suitability for your child. Find out the make to check that it is reasonably valued. When working on a budget for the pony, always remember to consider the cost of all the equipment you will need.

Vetting

Vetting is a pre-purchase examination carried out by a vet to check the pony's heart, eyes, wind and soundness. There are two types of vetting: two stage and five stage. The five-stage vetting is more thorough, with

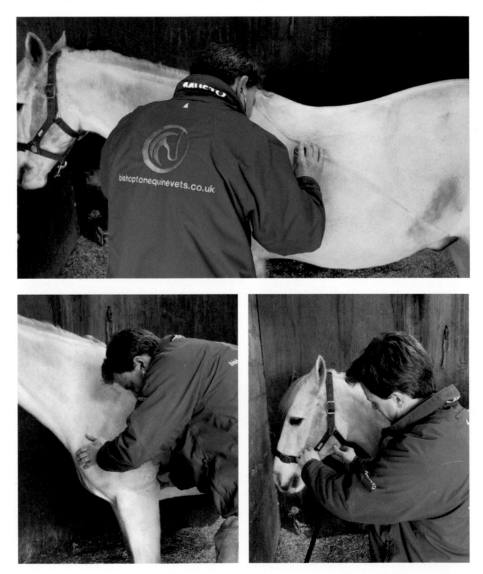

Top right: A pony being vetted.

Right: The vet checks the pony's heart.

Far right: Taking the pulse.

70

the horse being examined before and after exercise. This may also be followed up with x-rays of the limbs. The two-stage vetting is a more basic vetting, where the horse is checked at rest and the examination includes the mouth, eyes, heart and lungs. It is then trotted up on a hard surface to check for soundness. In both cases, a blood sample is taken for storage. If in the near future, after purchasing, the pony goes lame for no apparent reason, the blood can be tested for substances that might have masked a lameness at the time of vetting.

Vettings may cost from £75 to £250 depending on what type and how far the vet has to travel. It is advisable to use your own vet when possible, or one that is recommended. The owner's present veterinarian should not vet the pony.

Deciding whether or not to have the pony vetted will depend on how well you know or trust the present owner. For the level and type of work expected of a first pony, it may not be necessary if you have known the pony for a number of years. However, if you are relying on the honesty of a stranger, it may be worth having a two-stage vetting. This will give you peace of mind that he will likely pass the vet when the time comes to sell him on. It may also be necessary to have a vetting done if you are intending to insure him.

Payment and receipt

It must be agreed, before collecting the pony, how he is to be paid for. This could be cash on collection, cheque or bank transfer. In the case of the latter two, it is likely the seller will not let the pony leave the yard until the money is in the bank. It is important that you obtain a receipt for any method of payment.

Receipt requirements

- **Passport number**
- **Microchip (if applicable)**
- **Description of the pony**
- **Seller's details**
- **Buyer's details**
- **Amount paid**
- **Type of payment**
- **Seller's signature**
- **Buyer's signature**
- **Date.**

Handing over the passport.

Agreement

If possible, have a written agreement that the pony can be returned and a full refund given if the pony does not prove to be as sold. This would typically cover the pony for the first week as after this the seller could state that the pony didn't have the problem and that you have caused it. Honest sellers who have nothing to hide would usually agree to this as they are as keen to see the pony go to the right home as you are to get the right pony.

Insurance

Insuring your pony is not a legal requirement but it does have several benefits. There are many companies that offer pony insurance and it is important to look into each one closely to see who offers the best deal for you. It is also useful to seek advice from others who have had experience making claims.

Pony insurance can cover:

- In the event of theft or straying.
- In the event of death.
- For some vet fees.
- Third party liability.
- Personal accident.
- Saddlery and tack.
- Disposal.
- Trailers.

If you do intend to insure the pony, this should be done before he is collected to cover any incident that may occur when transporting him home.

Information regarding the pony

It is important to make a note of the following information relating to the pony's management:

- What feed he has been having.
- What bedding he is on.
- What amount of turnout he has had.
- Whether he is usually turned out alone or with others.
- When he was last shod, how often and any special requirements.
- Worming routine and when his next treatment is due.

- When his vaccinations are due (this should be checked in the passport).

- When he last saw the dentist.

- When he was last ridden.

- How much work he has been doing.

- Any other information they can offer that may help him settle and adjust to his new home.

6

Where to keep the pony

Careful consideration must be given as to where your new pony will live. This chapter looks at the options available and offers advice on what will work best for you.

Stabling at home

Keeping your pony at home is what most children dream of, waking up and being able to look out of their bedroom window and see the pony grazing in the paddock. In reality, this is only practical if you are lucky enough to have land, facilities and the experience to care for him.

The pony will need a paddock for turnout. The field should provide at least one acre per pony. If he is going to be living out full time then this should be doubled to allow the field to be split; one half can then

A pony living out.

be grazed while the other is rested. The field must also not be too big otherwise problems may occur with the pony overindulging or not willing to be caught..

If the pony is living out full time, the field will require a shelter. If this is not provided naturally by hedges and trees, a field shelter will need to be built.

A suitable field shelter.

Ideally, you should have a stable, even if you intend the pony to live out full time. This will give you a dry place to groom and tack up during the winter months. There may also be occasions when the pony will need to be stabled due to health issues.

It is also an advantage to have somewhere safe to ride the pony. At this stage of your child's riding career it is not necessary to have an Olympic-size arena, but an enclosed area where they can walk, trot and canter is an advantage. The field is as good as anywhere when the ground is suitable. Care must be taken in winter as it will quickly become poached. If you don't have these facilities, is there an arena within hacking distance that you can hire? Children and ponies enjoy hacking and improve tremendously from this. If you are located on a busy road, hacking is not ideal and this should be taken into consideration.

If the facilities are all in place, it must still be considered how much time, knowledge and experience you have to look after the pony. If both parents have full-time jobs, it may not be practical. If it is your intention to have the pony at home, it is important that you have the necessary training on stable management, especially feeding and pony health. Problems can very quickly escalate when not recognised early. Having an experienced person who lives locally is always an advantage. It must also be considered who will take care of the pony when you are not there.

While having the pony at home may initially be appealing to your child, you may find that the novelty soon wears off. This is often the case if the child is always doing things on their own. Usually they have much more pony fun when they are caring for and riding their pony with friends. Equally, not all ponies are happy living alone, as this is not natural for them. You may find that he is unsettled when ridden and in the stable or field. This can lead to issues with his condition and temperament. He may become naughty when ridden, causing your child to lose confidence and not want to ride. If you are in a position where you do have the facilities and adequate land, then it could be an option to take in another pony that could act as a companion. This would work really well if it also provided a friend for your child to ride with.

Having a friend to ride with adds to the enjoyment of having a pony.

Livery yards

If stabling at home is not an option, or not one you want to consider to begin with, then you need to look into keeping your pony at livery. This is when you pay to keep your pony on a commercial yard. Livery yards can vary in size, type, facilities and the services they offer.

Full livery

The yard's staff undertake all care of the horse or pony kept on full livery. This often includes exercise or training, if required. The advantage of this is that you do not need to worry about the management side whatsoever. The staff will organise the farrier, vet and dentist when necessary, as well as ordering feed, hay and bedding. The disadvantage is that you will spend much less time at the stables, therefore the child may not bond so well with their pony. It is also less likely that you will learn about and improve your stable management skills. Full livery is also the most expensive option and can be quite costly.

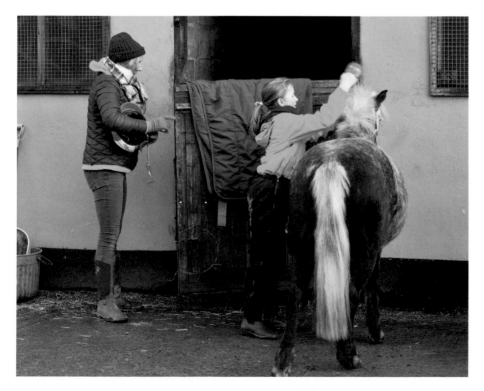

A pony on DIY livery.

DIY (do it yourself) livery

With this livery option, a stable and/or field is provided by the yard. This may or may not include bedding. All the stable duties are carried out by you, the owner. You will also be responsible for buying feed and hay as well as organising and being there for any farrier, vet or dentist visits. This type of livery requires you to be at the yard at least twice a day, which is obviously time consuming. It is not usually practical for the child to do this during school term time, therefore it becomes the responsibility of the parents. If time does allow, it is a much cheaper option and can be very enjoyable.

Part livery

On part livery, responsibility is shared between the staff and the pony's owner. Some yards may set the rules on what services they provide and what is the owner's responsibility. For example, the staff may feed and water, turn out and bring in, while mucking out, grooming and exercise are the owner's responsibility. Other yards may allow you to state what you would like to do. This usually works much better, especially if the arrangement can be flexible.

Working livery

This option is typically offered at riding schools. The pony is cared for by the staff and used by clients of the riding school. An advantage of this is that you are getting the full livery service at a discounted rate. The pony is also being worked on a regular basis. The disadvantage is that the pony may not always be available when you want him. The pony is also being ridden by lots of different children which may not be in his best interest. Riding school ponies can often become sour and bad tempered if overused.

What to look for in a livery yard

The location of the yard must be considered for several reasons. Firstly, it must be within a sensible travelling distance to make it practical to get to. Consider not only how long it will take to get there from home but also from work and school. Is the route affected by heavy traffic at certain times of the day? Will it be possible to get there if weather conditions are bad, such as ice and snow? It is also an advantage if the yard is located in a more rural area that can offer pleasant and safe hacking.

Viewing

For your requirements, the yard does not need to be super smart but it is important that it is safe and well maintained. Once you have found one in a suitable location, it is advisable to contact the owner or manager to ask relevant questions and arrange a viewing.

When viewing the yard, take note of the following.

Stables

Ask to be shown around the yard and then the stable that is available for you. This should be no smaller than 10ft by 10ft for a pony. It should be well ventilated and have decent drainage. Check in and outside the stable for anything that could be dangerous such as sharp objects, windows without bars, uncovered light bulbs or badly fitting fixtures. Take note of the watering system, feed manger, hayrack and tie-up rings.

QUESTIONS TO ASK AT LIVERY STABLES

◊ *What livery options are available?*

◊ *What are the costs?*

◊ *What facilities do they offer (and any conditions of use)?*

◊ *What turn out availability is there?*

◊ *What feed and/or bedding can be provided?*

◊ *How many horses are there on the yard?*

◊ *What type of clientele, children and ponies?*

◊ *What help and advice is available for stable management and riding?*

◊ *Is your own instructor allowed to teach?*

◊ *What insurance do they have?*

◊ *What insurance will you need?*

◊ *What storage space do they allow for tack and equipment?*

◊ *Do they have parking for horseboxes or trailers?*

◊ *What are the conditions regarding the farrier and veterinarian?*

◊ *Do they offer a clipping service?*

◊ *What hacking is available?*

◊ *What is their worming policy?*

◊ *Who lives on site?*

These must be safely fitted and at a suitable height for your pony; if they are not, ask if they can be adjusted.

Rubber floor mats are not essential but an advantage as they reduce the amount of bedding required and the risk of injury. Note where the stable is located in relation to other horses and ponies. Ask about the temperament of the potential neighbours. Do they have any vices? Are they sociable to both people and other horses? If possible, you want to avoid the risk of your child or pony being bitten or kicked. If you are interested in full or part livery, check to see if the bedding looks clean, the stables regularly skipped out, and if fresh water and hay are available. Do the horses or ponies that you see look happy and in a healthy condition? During your visit take note of the activity of the staff, their attitude towards you and how they handle the horses. Have a chat with as many of the staff as possible to get a feel of the working atmosphere. A well-run, happy yard will generate a good feeling.

Fields

Have a look at the grazing available and find out where your pony will be turned out. The field needs to be a suitable size; as mentioned, this should be at least one acre per pony. The fencing must be safe, post and

An unfriendly neighbour.

rail or hedges are ideal. Barbed wire or sheep netting are not suitable. Electric tape is acceptable to divide a field but should not be the main fencing. The gate should be well hung and open inwards. A clean source of water needs to be available in a large trough. This shouldn't be situated too close to the gate or under trees.

The amount of grass growing will depend on the time of year. Grass grows at its best during the spring and its feed value becomes very high. This is often a risk to ponies, as will be discussed in Chapter 10. If this is the case, it will be necessary to ask for a starvation paddock until the

Clockwise: Suitable post and rail fencing.

A good latch.

Electric fencing dividing a field.

A poached field.

QUESTIONS TO ASK ABOUT TURN OUT

◊ *How much turn out is available?*

◊ *Is it shared with other horses and ponies?*

◊ *Do they run mares and geldings separately?*

◊ *What is the policy on hind shoes being worn when turning out in company?*

◊ *Do the fields close during the winter, if so does this affect the cost of the livery?*

◊ *Is there a set time for turning out and bringing in? If not, how do they avoid ponies being left out alone?*

growth slows. In summer, grass doesn't grow as quickly and fields can often look over grazed or 'horse sick'. This can be avoided by good grassland management. In winter, fields can become very poached, especially around gateways. If over stocked, the poaching will spread and the paddock will resemble a ploughed field. For this reason, some yards may close the fields for a period over the winter. Will this suit your pony? Notice how many piles of droppings can be seen. Ideally, poo picking should be done daily to reduce the risk of worm infestation and prevent the field from looking horse sick. This is also a good chance to check for any poisonous plants, ragwort being the most common. The state of the paddocks often reflects the management of the yard.

Find out the terms and conditions of turnout by asking questions.

Tack room and storage areas

If the yard offers a tack room it must be well secured. It is important to be clear on the insurance policy. If they do not cover your equipment, it is advisable to get your own insurance. Have a look at the organisation of the tack room and how safe you think your equipment will be. Large yards are renowned for losing equipment as it needs good management to keep track of everything. Ask what the policy is on the hours that the tack room is open, as it is frustrating if you want to ride but the tack room is locked. Storage space should also be available for feed, hay

Above: Find out the policy on turn out.

Left: Storage for hay and straw.

QUESTIONS TO ASK ABOUT ARENAS

◊ *Is the use of the arena included in the livery cost?*

◊ *Is there an extra cost for the use of the lights?*

◊ *Does it need to be booked in advance?*

◊ *Are there set times it can be used?*

◊ *Do they have a maximum number of horses allowed in at one time?*

◊ *Is it possible to hire it for sole use?*

◊ *Is your own instructor allowed to teach you in the arena?*

◊ *What are the terms and conditions for using jump equipment?*

◊ *Does the arena cope with all weather conditions such as heavy rain or frost?*

QUESTIONS TO ASK ABOUT HORSE WALKERS

◊ *Is it included in the livery costs?*

◊ *Does it have to be booked?*

◊ *Is there a time limit?*

◊ *Can it be used all year round?*

and bedding. It should be noted how owners' supplies are identified and not used by others.

Arenas

Most larger livery yards will have an arena, if not several. Take a look at the safety of the arena and if the surface looks good. A well-maintained arena will be harrowed daily, watered if necessary, and any droppings will be removed. If this is not done it can quickly become a dangerous surface to ride on. Find out the terms and conditions of using the arena by asking questions.

Horse walker

Most larger yards will have a horse walker. This is very useful for giving the pony a leg stretch, providing exercise on days he can't be ridden or taking some of the freshness out of him. Find out the terms and conditions of using the horse walker by asking questions.

Hacking

Find out what hacking is available from the yard. Is it mostly on the road or are there bridle paths? Are the roads busy, if so is it mostly cars or heavier traffic such as lorries and tractors? Are there often other liveries hacking who wouldn't mind your child joining them? Are there routes that are suitable for you to accompany on a bike?

Above: Ensure you know the terms and conditions of arena use.

Left: Horse walker.

Existing clients

Try to visit the yard at a busy time and take the opportunity to speak to as many clients as possible. A weekend would be ideal as then hopefully you can meet other parents and children. It would be a more suitable choice if there are other children of a similar age and ability rather than a yard full of adults. If the yard has a waiting list it is a good sign. If it has more empty stables than full then this could indicate that it is not a good establishment. If a yard appeals to you but doesn't have space at the present time, it is worth being put on a waiting list and finding a temporary solution until a stable is available.

7

Bringing the pony home

Before bringing your pony to his new home it is important to be well prepared. If you have decided to keep him on a livery yard, discuss with the staff when would be a good time to arrive with him.

What you will need

- **Headcollar and rope**
- **Bridle**
- **Tail bandage**
- **Travel boots (optional)**
- **Bedding**
- **Hay/haylage**
- **Concentrates (optional)**
- **Feed buckets and feed scoop**
- **Water buckets**
- **Haynet (optional)**
- **Rugs (if necessary)**
- **Wheelbarrow, fork, shovel, broom and skip**
- **Basic grooming kit.**

Preparation

Choose a day when you know you have lots of time and, if possible, when your child can be there. It is not necessary to pre-purchase all the equipment you are going to need. It is often better to start with the essentials and buy extras as you progress. Seeing what others have and use can help you choose the most efficient and cost-effective equipment.

The saddle is not listed as this is not an item that you can walk into the shop, choose and buy. It needs to be fitted to the pony by a professional, as will be discussed in Chapter 12. The stable should be bedded down before the pony arrives, hay provided, and the water buckets ready to fill. If the stable has an automatic watering system this should be cleaned on the day of arrival.

You will need a place to tie up your pony, both inside and outside the stable. Many people make the mistake of trying to muck out and groom without doing this. The pony can quickly become bad mannered and the job can end up taking much longer. Ponies are renowned for being escape artists. Given the slightest opportunity, most will take the chance to leave the stable, usually heading for the closest patch of grass or the feed room. They often have little respect for anything or anyone in their way. When on a busy yard, with lots of equipment and children, this can become disruptive and dangerous. Tying up may take two

Above left: A stable is prepared.

Below: A pony gets loose.

minutes longer but in the end saves time, teaches good manners and avoids unnecessary disruption.

It is important that the pony is only ever tied to well-fitted tie-up rings. It can be tempting to attach him to other fittings, in and out of the stable, such as the bars on windows, stable doors and fencing. Avoid this when possible as even the strongest looking structure can break with the strength of a pony behind it.

A piece of bale string must be attached to the ring and the pony tied to this, rather than to the ring itself. The reason being, if the pony were to panic and try to get away, the ring itself would not allow this, resulting in the pony injuring himself as he is in danger of falling over or putting an enormous amount of strain on himself. When attached to the string, if he panics it will break if necessary. The string should be thinned slightly as often full thickness does not break quickly enough. An alternative to this is a specially designed 'quick-release' lead rope. This has a fastening that can manually be quickly undone. However, this is only useful if you are standing by the pony at the time, and is therefore not always suitable.

Above: String on a ring, like this, provides a suitable tying place for your pony.

Below left: Pony tied too short.

Below right: Pony tied too long.

The tie-up ring should be at the correct height for the pony to be tied in a comfortable, safe position. If too high, he will find it uncomfortable

and will be more likely to resist. If too low, there is a danger of him putting a foot over the rope. A quick-release knot must always be used. It is important that your child is shown how to do this.

Above: Teaching how to do the quick-release knot.

Left: Not a suitable place to tie up.

Transport

It will be necessary to arrange transport for your pony. It is not advisable to do this yourself if you have little experience dealing with ponies, towing a trailer or driving a horsebox. In some cases, the seller may offer to bring the pony to you. This way, they can see the new home which can offer some comfort. If not, a friend may step in to help and bring the pony home for you.

Failing this, there are many commercial transport companies. This is often a better option if the pony has a long journey. They are highly experienced in travelling with horses and ponies and will ensure your pony is well cared for during the trip. It will not be necessary for you to be present.

If collecting the pony in person, it will be necessary to take a correctly fitting headcollar, rope and tail bandage. Take the bridle in case there is a problem loading. Discuss with the seller what other equipment the pony would usually travel in. He may also need travel boots and a rug. For all the pony's clothing, seek the seller's advice on what size to purchase as ill-fitting equipment can lead to rubs and sores.

It is advisable to collect the pony in daylight and allow enough travel time to arrive at his new home before dark. The seller will usually be present to hand the pony over along with any equipment and, most importantly, his passport. This is often a very distressing time for the child, if not the whole family, who are letting him go. Patience is needed to give them time to say goodbye. Reassure the seller that you will stay in touch, send lots of photos and that they are welcome to come and see him. Hopefully, this won't lead to them constantly calling you; usually, when their next pony is found they will detach themselves.

Arrival

On arrival home, unload the pony and take him to his new stable. Remove all his clothing and allow him to familiarise himself with his

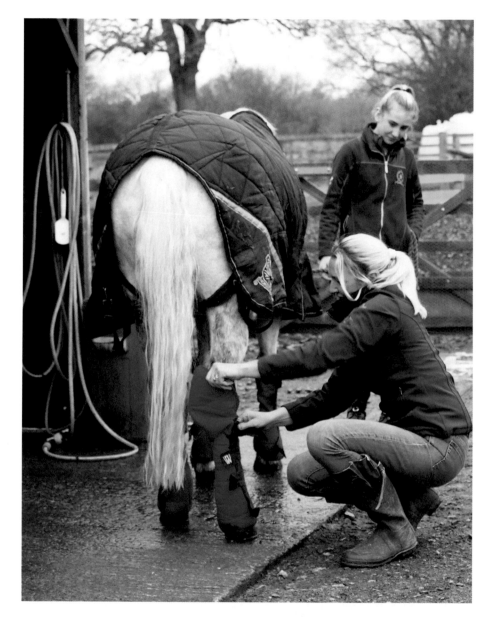

Pony arrives at new home.

new surroundings. At this stage, give him time alone but observe his behaviour. It is expected that an older, well-travelled pony will settle quickly and be undeterred by the move. He will display this by tucking into the food available, maybe having a roll and generally looking relaxed. If, however, he is not interested in food, is box walking or has his head out whinnying and looking stressed, then he is going to take more time to settle.

Introduction to the field

When to turn out for the first time will depend on how well the pony has settled in the stable. If he is totally relaxed, he could be turned out on the first day. If he is used to being out on his own then it is advisable to start this way. If he is going to share a field with a number of other ponies, it may be best to turn him out with just one or two individuals before he joins the herd.

Don't attempt to turn out the pony until he is more settled in the stable as there is a risk he will gallop around and injure himself or unsettle others. An experienced adult can lead the pony out and let him hand graze. Hopefully, once he becomes more familiar with his surroundings, he will settle. This behaviour is more typical of a young pony and not an older schoolmaster.

Hand grazing.

*Getting to know
your new pony.*

Riding

As soon as you have your pony home, it is likely your child will want to ride. It is not advisable to be in a hurry to do so as it could all too quickly go wrong. Let the pony have the first day to settle in. Time can be spent grooming and getting to know him on the ground. If possible, arrange for

97

your instructor to be present for the first ride. If at this point you don't yet have a saddle, this may have to wait unless it is possible to borrow a suitable one that fits.

The first ride should be in a safe, enclosed area under supervision. Even the most bombproof pony may react differently in a new environment, and it should not be taken for granted that he will behave as he did when you tried him. If the pony looks nervous and unsettled, it is advisable to lunge him first or have a more experienced child ride him. Again, it is usual that the pony will settle in a day or two. If the nervous behaviour continues, discuss this with his previous owner as this is the time the pony can be classed as 'not sold as seen' and returned.

The first week of owning the pony should be about settling in and getting to know him. Riding should be very low key and more time should be spent in the stable with him. Good management from here on is essential if the pony is going to maintain the good behaviour he came with. The book's remaining chapters offer advice on all aspects of care, management and dealing with problems that may occur.

8
Daily routine

Horses and ponies thrive on routine and it is an essential part of good stable management. If the pony is kept on full or part livery, it is likely the yard will run to a routine.

Examples of a yard's daily routine	
7am	Feed concentrates
7am	Muck out and put pony on horse walker
9am	Fill haynets, prepare feeds, tidy yard
10am	Exercise
12 noon	Turn out in paddock, skip out stable
5pm	Bring in and groom
6pm	Feed and hay
6.30pm	Feed and hay

The routine may vary for different horses and ponies, some may be turned out in the morning and exercised in the afternoon, others may have longer turnout. In summer it is common to turn out overnight and bring in during the day, the horse then avoids the heat and flies.

The above routine is a typical example but not always practical for someone looking after their own pony, as it does require you to be on the yard most of the day. Whatever routine you choose, it is important to stick to it as much as possible as the pony will be happier if he knows what to expect each day. The routine may change at the weekends and during school holidays to suit your child. This is fine, but whenever possible try to keep feed times the same and give the pony the same amount of time in the field.

Below is an example of a daily routine for a DIY livery or a pony living at home.

Example of a daily routine for a DIY livery or pony living at home	
7am	Feed
7am	Turn out
8–9am	School run
9am	Muck out and do stable duties
4pm	Child home from school. Bring pony in to groom and ride
5pm	Put pony to bed, feed and hay

It may be necessary during the spring and summer months to limit the grazing; the pony may have to come in earlier unless a starvation paddock is available. How the pony is cared for will very much depend on whether he is living in or out.

Living out

Having your pony live out has many advantages. It is much more natural for him than being stabled, therefore he should benefit both mentally and physically. His diet replicates that of being in his natural environment and he has plenty of fresh air and exercise. These factors will contribute to him being healthy and more relaxed when ridden.

The costs are also obviously going to be much less than those of a stabled pony. However, if the grass-kept pony is not managed well, you may face a large vet bill. For example, weight control can be an issue. Ponies living out can easily become too fat in spring and summer, putting them at risk of laminitis (see Chapter 10). Conversely, older ponies may lose too much weight during the winter months. Mud fever and cracked heels are another common problem in winter when the fields become very wet and poached. Catching and riding from the field is not as easy as having your pony in the stable, more so in the winter months when he will be covered in mud and grooming can be quite time consuming.

Care of the grass-kept pony

Keeping your pony at grass does not mean you can abandon him from one weekend to the next. He must be checked daily, along with the field he is living in.

Ponies living out.

Visit the pony at least once a day. Take a general look over him to check he has no obvious injuries and make sure you see him on the move to check for soundness. Picking out his feet on a regular basis will give you a chance to check his shoes and prevent a build-up of mud and stones which can cause disease and lameness.

During the winter months, the pony may be prone to rain scald, a skin condition that causes scabs to form, mainly on the hindquarters, which can then spread to the back under the saddle. It may be necessary to apply a New Zealand rug to prevent this. The rug should be removed daily to check that it is not rubbing at the shoulder or withers. It is also essential to closely monitor the pony's weight as condition can be lost rapidly in winter.

Above: Feet should be picked out daily.

Left: A field shelter is an advantage.

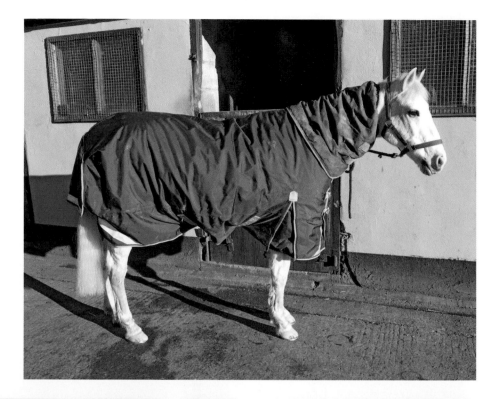

Right: A New Zealand rug.

Below left: A fly mask.

Below right: Sun cream applied.

During the summer, the pony may need protection against the flies. Fly spray works for a limited period and is not very effective, therefore he may need a fly sheet. If his eyes are runny or swollen he will benefit from wearing a fly mask, which can be removed at night. Ponies that have pink skin around their lips and muzzle are at high risk of sunburn, so it is essential that sun cream is applied frequently on sunny days.

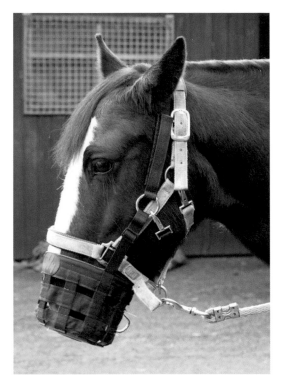

It is important to monitor the pony's weight. It can be difficult to assess weight gain or loss when seeing the pony daily. Ask the opinion of your instructor when she sees the pony for a lesson. During spring, it is essential that care is taken to avoid the risk of weight gain and laminitis. If a starvation paddock is not available, it is necessary to apply a grazing muzzle for part of the day.

Grooming

Before riding your pony, he will need to be groomed to remove the worst of the mud from him in order to prevent rubs and sores from occurring. However, he will need to keep the natural oils in his coat to protect him against the wet. A dandy brush or plastic curry comb should therefore be used rather than a body brush. His feet should be picked out and his eyes, nose and dock cleaned with separate damp sponges.

Above: A grazing muzzle.

Left: Using the rubber curry comb.

Feeding

During the winter months, it may be necessary to feed the pony in the field as the grass will have very little feed value. Hay or haylage tends to be sufficient for most ponies. Very old ponies may struggle to eat hay due to tooth deterioration, which naturally occurs with age, and may therefore require a suitable concentrate feed.

When feeding in the field try to avoid waste, often hay will be trampled into the mud. Place it in a sheltered spot away from the gate. Putting it in a large container is helpful. If feeding a number of ponies, it is important to avoid conflict between them and ensure that individuals at the bottom of the pecking order get their fair share. This is done by spreading out small piles around an area. There should always be at least two more piles than there are ponies. The dominant ponies will constantly move from pile to pile but this should ensure they are all fed. Feeding in the herd can often cause ponies to become aggressive, for this reason children should not be present in the field at feeding time.

Below left: Hay feeder.

Below right: Dirty water trough.

The field must also be checked over daily. Fencing should be intact and any repairs should be carried out immediately to avoid further damage,

escape or risk of injury. The gate should be well maintained and not allowed to drop or become difficult to open and close.

Water must be checked daily and cleaned when necessary. Ponies will drink much more in summer time than in winter. Therefore, if filled manually, it will need topping up twice daily. During cold weather, the trough may freeze and will need the ice breaking.

The field should be poo picked on a regular basis, ideally daily. This is also a good opportunity to check for poisonous plants growing in the field or hedgerows. Anything that is pulled up should immediately be removed as it can still be poisonous when dead. It is essential that you and your child are familiar with poisonous plants and, if not, research should be done.

Care of the stabled pony

Having your pony stabled all the time is not advisable as he is likely to become bored and extremely fresh, causing bad manners when handled and ridden. A partly stabled pony does, however, have advantages as he can be more easily monitored, kept cleaner and is less likely to develop injuries and skin problems. More time will be spent with him which will encourage a stronger relationship between child and pony. Most children enjoy caring for their pony as much as riding him.

Bedding

The stable will need some form of bedding to prevent injury and encourage the pony to soil and lay down. Straw is the cheapest and most common bedding to use. It is usually easy to come across and can be bought in small bales that are easy to transport. Wheat and barley straw are the most commonly used. It is important that the straw is clean and free of mould as this may cause the pony to cough. Eating straw is harmless to the pony unless consumed in large amounts. This would only be likely if the pony has been starved for some reason and then put onto a straw bed. A very greedy pony may overindulge causing him to gain weight, making it necessary to use a different type of bedding. Shavings are the most common alternative to straw. This is a much more expensive option and only necessary if your pony cannot be on straw for some reason.

Mucking out

Your stable should be mucked out daily. This entails removing the droppings and soiled straw, the clean bedding can be moved to the side and the floor swept. The stable is then bedded down and new straw added if necessary. If the pony is out through the day it is advantageous to leave the bed up to allow the floor to dry before bedding down again. When the pony is in, he should be skipped out as frequently as possible to avoid the droppings mixing with the clean straw.

Mucking out.

Grooming

Grooming your pony is a great way to spend time with him and get to know him better. Most ponies appreciate the experience and children tend to enjoy doing it. It is also essential as it keeps the coat and skin healthy and gives you a chance to check over the pony for any cuts, lumps or bumps. Your child will need a basic grooming kit to start with. This can then be added to as time goes on.

Items in a grooming kit

- **Suitable container for storage**
- **Hoof pick**
- **Dandy brush**
- **Body brush**
- **Rubber curry comb**
- **Metal curry comb**
- **Mane and tail brush**
- **Sponges × 2**
- **Stable rubber/ grooming mitt.**

The grooming kit.

Grooming routine

The pony should be tied up in a safe place where he will stand quietly and relaxed. Grooming should be an enjoyable experience for both pony and child but can be a chore if the pony is unsettled and does not want to stand still.

From an early age, it is advantageous if your child learns to groom in an orderly manner. This makes the procedure more effective and ensures areas are not missed. The following routine is for a stabled pony, it may differ slightly depending on the time of year and thickness of the coat. It can take up to forty minutes if done thoroughly but this is not necessary every day.

Feet

Any grooming session should start with the feet being picked out. This enables you to clean and check the condition of the hoof, frog and shoes. The hoof pick is used to displace mud and dirt. Always work from the heel to the toe and avoid pressure on the frog as it is a very sensitive structure. The foot should not smell offensive or the frog appear too moist. Run an eye over the shoe to check it has not twisted. A stiff brush can be used to clean the frog. The hoof should be cool to touch, if it feels hot compare it with the others. If all feel the same then the pony is likely to be warm, but if one foot has more heat than the others, this could be an indicator that he is harbouring a problem. The feet should be scrubbed out at least once a week using warm water and a mild disinfectant. This will help prevent thrush, a bacterial infection, which will be discussed in more detail in Chapter 10.

Picking out the feet.

Removing mud

The next step is to remove any mud from the coat, to do this effectively it must be dry. The dandy brush or plastic curry comb are the most suitable grooming utensils for this. The plastic curry comb works better on heavier mud and thicker coats, as it can be used in a backwards and forwards motion to loosen the mud. The dandy brush has stiff bristles and is designed to be used on thick coats only. Short strokes are the most effective at doing the job. Care must be taken with both these utensils when grooming the sensitive areas, such as the legs and belly. If the pony starts to show signs of irritation, such as tail swishing or laying his ears back, it is better to use something softer such as a hessian grooming mitt. If the pony has mud on his

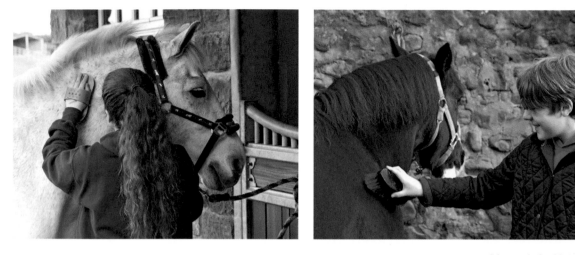

face, it is essential he is untied before attempting to groom. The plastic curry comb can be gently used but if he is at all worried, the hessian grooming mitt is a better option.

Above left: Using the plastic curry comb.

Removing grease

Once the pony is mud free, the next step is to groom the mane, neck, body, and legs. This entails bringing grease to the surface of the coat using the rubber curry comb and removing it with the body brush.

Above right: The dandy brush.

Below: The rubber curry comb.

The rubber curry comb can be used on large surface areas such as the neck, back and hindquarters. It can be used under the belly, if the pony is not too sensitive and will tolerate it, and on the face and upper leg region if heavy pressure is avoided. It is used in a circular motion, increasing the pressure once you know the pony is happy. Grease will soon appear on the surface of the coat. This will be less effective on very thick coat, but is still worth

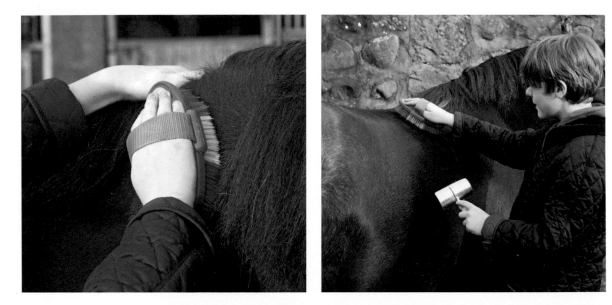

Top left: Brushing
the mane.

Top right: The
body brush and
metal curry comb.

Right: Cleaning
the metal curry
comb.

doing as it helps to increase the circulation. Clipped ponies benefit less from this and using a hot cloth is a more effective method (see Chapter 14). The rubber curry comb is also very useful for removing loose hair when the pony is moulting.

The body brush can then be used to remove the grease. This is a soft-bristled brush and suitable for all areas. The metal curry comb

Brushing the face with the pony untied.

is used to clean the body brush between strokes. Start by brushing through the mane, here grease accumulates underneath and at the roots. The mane should be brushed over to the opposite side, it can then be split and groomed in sections, ensuring you get as close to the crest as possible. Next, work from the neck down to the chest and foreleg, then to the body, tummy, hindquarters and, finally, the hind leg. The body brush should be held in the hand closest to the pony and metal curry comb in the other. Use long strokes for larger areas and smaller strokes for tricky parts. Frequently scrape the brush with the metal curry comb, which can be banged on the floor to clean it. The same procedure is then repeated on the other side. It provides quite a strenuous workout and is a great form of exercise. The face can then be groomed using either the body brush or a smaller face brush. The pony must be untied to do this, the headcollar can be undone and placed around the neck to allow a more thorough job.

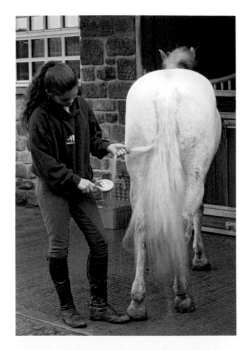

Tail

The top of the tail will become very greasy and the bottom will get muddy during the winter months. Use the body brush at the top to remove the grease.

Part the hairs and get as close to the dock as possible. The bottom can be brushed out using a tail brush if it is clean and tangle free. Doing it this way when knotty will result in pulling out a lot of hair and you will very quickly have a pony with a thin tail. If this is the

Right: Grooming the tail.

Below: Final touches with the grooming mitt.

case, avoid using a brush and use your fingers to remove bedding. When preparing for a competition or Pony Club, the tail can be washed and conditioner applied to make it easier to brush and avoid splitting the hair.

Eyes, nose and dock

The eyes and nostrils should then be cleaned with a damp sponge. Again, always untie to do this. The sponge should be cleaned afterwards. A separate sponge is used to clean under the tail. Stand to the side to do this, never directly behind, as you may get kicked.

Final touches

To finish the grooming session, the coat can be given a final polish using the stable rubber or soft grooming mitt. Gently wipe over the entire pony. Follow this by laying the mane onto the side that it naturally lies on, using a wet water brush to dampen it if necessary. If the hooves are dry and clean, a dressing can be applied to help keep them healthy.

Bathing

Bathing your pony is a good way to get the coat thoroughly clean. This should only be done in suitable weather unless your yard is equipped with warm water and heat lamps to help dry the pony and prevent him catching a chill. It may be necessary to give your pony a bath to help with skin problems or to prepare him for a competition. Bathing too often will reduce the natural oils in the coat, therefore once a week is usually sufficient. Avoid bathing ponies that live out without rugs, as the grease offers protection against wet weather.

Before starting to bathe, it is advisable to have all the necessary equipment ready. Warm water is more effective at cleaning the coat and kinder in colder weather.

Equipment

- **Buckets × 2**
- **Sponges × 2**
- **Shampoo**
- **Sweat scraper**
- **Towels**
- **Rugs.**

Equipment

Not all ponies take too kindly to having a bath and may be more difficult to handle than usual. Ensure they are tied up in a safe area and the equipment is close at hand but is not going to be knocked over. It may be necessary to have someone hold him if he is really not enjoying the procedure.

To introduce the hosepipe, run the water next to the pony until he is comfortable with the sound. It is advisable to have someone hold the pony until you are confident he is not going to panic. Once he relaxes, run the hose over a front hoof and gradually make your way up the leg to the shoulder. If he continues to be happy with this, the hose can be used to wet the mane and body. If he is not too keen, it is safer to use a bucket and sponge.

Start by wetting the mane. Once thoroughly wet, shampoo can be added and massaged into the crest. This should then be thoroughly rinsed. Next, starting at the top of the neck, wet the body and legs, then shampoo both sides. Once the shampoo is applied, a soft brush or rubber curry comb can be used to get deeper into the coat. The shampoo should

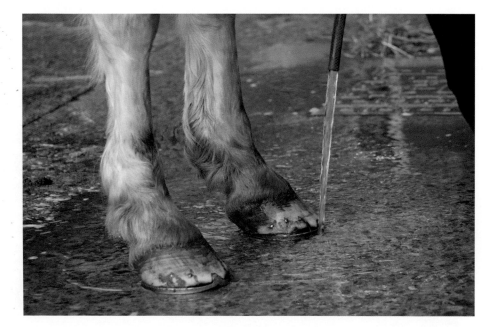

Introducing the hosepipe.

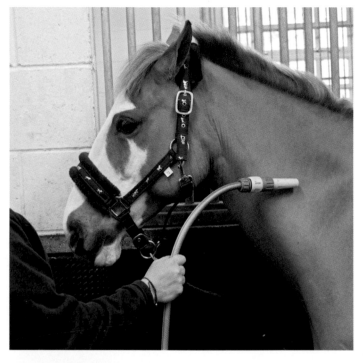

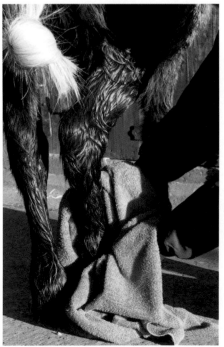

Clockwise: A pony not keen on having his face washed.

Make sure the pony is happy with the hosepipe before washing the neck and mane.

Washing the tail.

Towel drying the legs.

then be rinsed out. Use the sweat scraper to remove as much water as possible. On a sunny day, the pony can be tied up and left to dry. If it is a colder day, a cooler rug should be applied to prevent the pony getting cold.

The tail can be washed next by placing it in a bucket or wetting with the hosepipe. Shampoo should be applied and worked into a lather. Extra attention should be paid to the dock area, which can become very greasy. Thoroughly rinse and shake out the excess water from the tail. The head is the last area to wash and can be the most tricky. Always untie the pony to do this. Avoid using a hosepipe as water may get into the ears and can cause the pony to become very distressed and much

Folding the rug forward.

more difficult next time. Apply a small amount of shampoo to the sponge and gently wash, taking care to avoid the eyes. The soap can be rinsed out and the head towel dried. The legs can also be rubbed with a towel to remove excess water. This is more important on white legs, which are more prone to developing skin problems. The mane should be brushed over to the correct side and the tail brushed out. If the tail is very thick and knotty, it will help to apply a tail conditioner. A tail bandage can be put on to help lay the tail neatly.

If it is necessary to bathe in very cold weather, a rug can be left on and the pony bathed in halves to help prevent him getting chilly. The rug can be folded back over the hindquarters while the mane, neck and back are

Folding the rug back.

done. Once rinsed and scraped, the process can be repeated over the hindquarters and the rugs folded forward. Dry rugs can then be put on before the legs, tail and head are done. In cold weather, avoid washing a pony that has a thick coat as it will take a long time to dry and the pony is likely to get very cold.

The pony can be put on a horse walker to dry, if one is available. Avoid putting him back in the stable or the field until the coat is totally dry, as he will more than likely want to roll. Once the coat is dry, clean rugs can be applied if required.

9
Feeding

Incorrect feeding is all too often the reason that a pony becomes naughty or unhealthy. 'Kill him with kindness' often applies as ponies generally survive well on very little. However, it is very easy to feel sorry for a hungry pony and be tempted to indulge him. Knowing the rules of feeding will help you understand why things are done in a certain way, and what is good and bad for the pony.

The following rules apply for horses and ponies. At times, certain things need to be modified for a pony.

1 Feed according to height, weight, type, age, temperament, workload and capability of rider.

An average horse or pony should be fed approximately 2 per cent of his body weight. This includes roughage and concentrates. Grass

An obese pony.

cannot be weighed, therefore the amount of time the horse is out and the quality of the grass must be accounted for. A horse who is in hard work or needing to gain weight will require 2.5 per cent of his body weight. A pony in good condition and doing very little work may only require 1.5 per cent of his body weight.

The type of feed you choose will depend on the pony's temperament. Is he lazy and requiring more energy or is he sharp and whizzy? A novice or unconfident rider will not benefit from sitting on a pony that has been fed too much or incorrectly.

2   Clean fresh water should be available at all times.

3   Provide plenty of roughage in the diet. This will help prevent digestive problems occurring.

A pony in good condition.

4 Feed by weight not volume.

5 Feed little and often. The horse has a very small stomach, about the size of a rugby ball. Naturally he is a trickle feeder, meaning he eats little and often, keeping his stomach about two-thirds full. Giving large amounts of food infrequently can cause colic.

6 Make changes of feed gradual. When feed types are suddenly changed microbes in the large intestine do not have time to adapt, which can result in loose droppings or colic.

7 Do not perform hard exercise for at least one hour after feeding concentrates as digestive problems can occur.

8 Always feed good quality concentrates and forage. Poor quality feed is a false economy and can lead to digestive and respiratory problems.

9 Keep all feeding and water utensils clean. Always remove uneaten food before adding fresh.

Suitable diet

Incorrect feeding is one of the prime causes of health problems and bad behaviour. This is often done through ignorance or being given the wrong advice. Feeding the child's pony is very different to feeding a horse in full work, therefore it is essential to listen to the right person.

Most Pony Club ponies will need nothing more than grass and good quality hay. A feed balancer containing vitamins and minerals may be needed during the winter or for the older pony. When the child is expecting a bit more from the pony, for example a week at camp or during holidays, it may be necessary to introduce low-energy concentrates.

When feeding ponies always err on the side of caution. The pony should be fed only hay when he arrives at his new home. Once he has settled and is riding nicely, other feed can be considered if felt necessary. This is rarely required at this stage.

The amount of hay the pony needs will depend on his weight, how much grass he is getting and the time of year. In winter, the grass has very little feed value and the pony will be burning more calories in order to cope with colder weather, especially if he is living out. A plump or overweight pony should receive 1.5 per cent of his body weight and one that is the correct weight should receive 2 per cent. Body weight can be measured using a weighbridge or tape. Livery yards will often have a feed rep visit who brings a weighbridge with them. The pony can be weighed and the feed rep will advise you on what to feed. If this is not available, your instructor can help you use a weigh tape. They should also be able to advise you on whether the pony looks too thin, fat or in good condition.

A pony being weighed on a weighbridge while a feed rep offers advice.

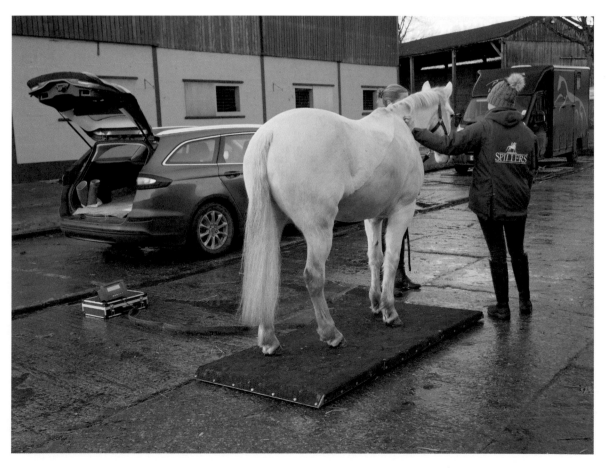

Average weight and feed guide		
9hh to 12.2hh	= 200kg at 2%	= 4kg of feed/day
12.3hh to 13.2hh	= 300kg at 2%	= 6kg of feed/day
13.3hh to 14.2hh	= 400kg at 2%	= 8kg of feed/day

Below left: Haynet being hung up.

Below middle: A clearly presented feed chart.

Below right: Hay being weighed.

Hay

The hay should be weighed in a bag or haynet before being divided into smaller portions to be fed during the day, and a slightly larger portion for the night. The day-time portions should be reduced if the pony is turned out on grass.

Haylage

Sometimes there is confusion over the difference between hay and haylage, and which is the most suitable to feed. Hay is cut and left to dry before being baled. Haylage is cut but only allowed to semi-wilt before it is baled and wrapped. The feed value of haylage is usually much higher than hay. For this reason, it is a more suitable source of roughage for horses in hard work and can often give ponies too much energy.

Concentrates

It may be necessary to feed concentrates if the pony is in poor condition or lacking sufficient energy for the work he is doing. In the case of a child's first pony, it may be that he is older and has problems with his teeth which prevent him eating enough roughage. Advice should be sought from your instructor or a feed rep as to the most suitable concentrate food for your pony. It is not advisable to try a feed without this advice as the wrong feed can have a dramatic effect on energy levels.

Top: Hay (on the left) and haylage (on the right).

Above: Feeds being mixed.

Obese ponies

Ponies often become overweight due to bad management. Native breeds especially tend to be very 'good doers' and practically live on fresh air. Being naturally greedy, they will constantly be telling their owner how

127

hungry they are! It can be tempting to feed them more than necessary as you feel sorry for them. However, this does them no favours and puts their health at risk. Using haynets with very small holes will slow down the pony's eating and make his roughage last longer. When grass is lush it may be necessary to reduce the grazing time or the quality of grazing. Fencing off a starvation paddock is a better option than stabling for longer hours as the pony is free to move around and will become less bored or fresh.

Purchasing

Hay can often be bought straight from the farmer. This will be cheaper than a supplier. The yard manager or livery owners will offer you advice on where the best deal can be found. Do not be tempted to go for poor quality to reduce costs. Dusty or mouldy forage will cause respiratory problems and even the greediest ponies will turn their noses up at it. Hay can often be delivered if the order is large enough, saving time and money. Try to share a load with other owners when possible.

Concentrates can be purchased at most saddlery or country stores. Again, ask for advice on the cheapest as there can be quite a difference in price. Large yards may order and have feed delivered for you. With all types of feed it is important to plan ahead and have new stock in before you run out.

Storage

Hay must be stored in a dry shed. If it is rained on and allowed to get wet it will become mouldy and inedible. Concentrate feed must be stored in a lidded bin to prevent it becoming damp and attracting vermin.

10
Pony health

Keeping your pony healthy is of utmost importance.
A better understanding of the signs of good health will enable you to recognise symptoms at an early stage. This can prevent a condition getting worse, causing the pony undue suffering and a large vet bill.

Signs of a healthy pony

When you first acquire your pony it is important to get to know him physically and mentally, and be able to recognise his normal temperament when ridden and in the stable. Getting to know him physically means you are aware of any blemishes he may already have. These are more commonly found on the lower legs, below the knee and hock, and may be in the form of swellings or scars. If the pony has been vetted you will have received a report stating any existing blemishes. The vet will also have discussed his findings with you and any implications on future

Lying down can be a sign of being off colour.

health issues. Take the time to look closely over your pony and feel his legs to identify these blemishes. If the pony wasn't vetted, it is advisable to do this with a more experienced person.

Ponies have varied personalities. Some are extroverts and like to have their head out over the stable door, always looking bright and alert. Others are more introverted and tend to spend more time at the back of the stable, minding their own business. It is important to note your pony's preference as a change in this could be an indication all is not well. Below are signs of good health that should be checked on a daily basis.

Morning checks

Before feeding, observe how your pony greets you. Most ponies will be looking out over the stable door eagerly awaiting breakfast. If this is his normal behaviour and you find your pony is lying down or standing at the back of the stable, the chances are he is not 100 per cent.

Check his bed is in the usual state, not more or less tidy than normal, and that he has passed the usual amount of droppings of the right consistency. Check sufficient water has been drunk and that the pony has eaten his feed and hay from the night before.

Does he look generally comfortable in himself with no obvious signs of lameness? If any of the above does not look normal it is advisable to investigate further.

TPR (temperature, pulse and respiration)

It is advantageous to know the normal temperature, pulse and respiration ranges as it is an indicator of when you might need to call the vet.

Temperature

A normal temperature is 37.5–38.5°C. This should only be taken by an experienced person as there is a high risk of being kicked.

When grooming your pony check for the following

- **Eyes are bright and free of discharge**

- **Nose is clean**

- **Gums are salmon pink (not pale)**

- **Glands are not swollen**

- **Skin is not dry and scurfy**

- **Skin is loose and supple. To test, pinch the skin on the neck, when you let go it should quickly flatten**

- **Coat has a healthy shine**

- **Legs feel cool and no new cuts or swellings**

- **Feet feel cool**

- **Skin is free from sores and rubs, especially in the saddle and bridle area.**

Taking the temperature.

Pulse

Normal range is 30–40 beats per minute. Again, it will take an experienced person to find the pulse. The sick pony is likely to display other symptoms that may be easier to recognise.

Respiration

Normal range is 8–15 breaths per minute. This is easier to assess and can be a useful indicator. Observe the movement of the flanks, in and out is one breath.

Count the breaths for 30 seconds and double the number to give you breaths per minute. All readings must be taken when the pony is at total rest and at least half an hour after exercise.

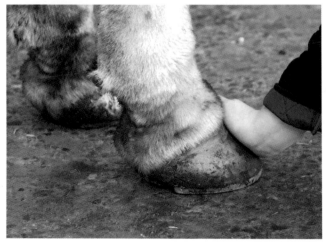

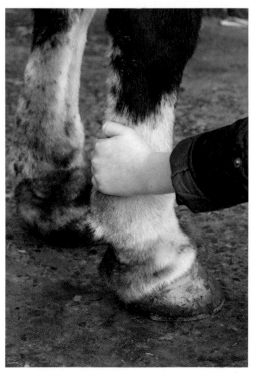

Clockwise from top left: Swollen glands.

Salmon pink gums.

Checking the hoof for heat.

Checking the leg for heat and swelling.

Common ailments

Caring for your pony does not require you to be the vet, but it is important that you are able to identify symptoms and know the correct procedure to deal with a problem. It is inevitable that at some point your pony will suffer from an ailment. Knowing the more common conditions and recognising early symptoms will enable you to act quickly.

Colic (abdominal pain)

Symptoms

◊ Rolling or lying down.
◊ Kicking the belly with a hind leg.
◊ Turning the head and neck to look at the belly.
◊ Pawing the ground.
◊ Lack of appetite.
◊ Lack of droppings.
◊ Increase in TPR.
◊ Sweating.
◊ Anxiety or depression.

Causes

There are several types of colic. Listed below are the three most common. Some of the causes are unavoidable but others are very much caused by bad management.

◊ Impaction – a blockage in the intestines, commonly caused by dehydration.
◊ Spasmodic – a build-up of gas in the gut due to fermentation, often caused by a change in diet or lack of roughage.
◊ Twisted gut – the intestines become twisted and can eventually cut off their blood supply. This is the most serious type of colic and will require surgery.

Treatment

◊   Remove all food.
◊   Check the horse is not too warm or cold.
◊   Try to prevent him rolling if he is going to injure himself further.
◊   Allow him to lie down if doing so quietly.
◊   If symptoms are mild allow him to hand graze.
◊   If symptoms persist or worsen within twenty minutes, call the vet immediately.
◊   If possible, take the temperature and respiration. Record droppings passed in the last six hours or overnight.
◊   The vet will need to know about the pony's appetite, any changes to his diet and if he has been wormed recently.
◊   If the vet is needed, he or she will carry out an assessment to ascertain the type of colic and treat accordingly. It is crucial to follow up their advice on treatment in the next forty-eight hours.

Prevention

Colic cannot always be prevented but good stable management plays a huge role.

Laminitis

Laminitis is a crippling condition of the hooves which can be fatal. It is very common in ponies and highly important that all pony owners are able to recognise the early symptoms.

Symptoms

Acute

Symptoms will come on very suddenly. The pony will be reluctant to walk and may lie down. He will be very lame, often in both front feet. The feet will be hot with a strong digital pulse. When standing, the pony will try to shift his weight onto his heels to relieve the pain from his toes.

Chronic

This is less dramatic, the pony will have ongoing symptoms as a result of a relapse from a previous attack. The toes often grow quicker than the heels and the hoof may show growth rings. Laminitic ponies also often develop a huge crest.

Causes

◊ High intake of sugars and starch, often caused by incorrect feeding or too much grass.
◊ Can follow other illnesses such as colic or infection.
◊ Cushing's disease.
◊ Trauma.
◊ Stress caused by change of environment or travelling.
◊ Mares are susceptible after foaling.
◊ Obesity.

Treatment

◊ Call the vet immediately.
◊ If possible, move the pony to a stable with a shavings bed. If the bedding packs into the hoof it will provide some support.

An overweight pony.

◊ Remove all food. Water should be available.
◊ Keep the pony as stress free as possible until the vet arrives.
◊ The vet will administer drugs to alleviate the pain.
◊ Follow the vet's advice on aftercare, this will include informing your farrier as the pony may require special shoeing.

Prevention

◊ Low sugar/starch diet.
◊ Limited grazing.
◊ Avoid the pony becoming overweight.
◊ Regular exercise.

Equine influenza

This is a common virus that affects the respiratory system and can lead to bacterial infection.

Symptoms

◊ Raised temperature lasting for one to three days.
◊ Enlarged glands.
◊ Loss of appetite.
◊ Depression.
◊ Dry cough.
◊ Nasal discharge which can be thick, yellow or green in colour.
◊ Swollen legs.

Treatment

◊ This condition is highly contagious and is likely to spread throughout the yard. If symptoms are recognised early and the pony can be isolated this may be prevented.
◊ Plenty of fresh air. The more the pony is out in the field grazing, the quicker he recovers.
◊ Complete rest for one to two weeks.

◊ The vet may need to prescribe antibiotics if a secondary bacterial infection occurs.
◊ Disinfect all equipment, especially feed and water buckets.
◊ Monitor the temperatures of all other horses on the yard.

Prevention

Young horses or ponies that are frequently transported and mixing with others are more susceptible. Vaccination is the best form of prevention and often compulsory for those that are competing or attending Pony Club activities.

A pony being vaccinated.

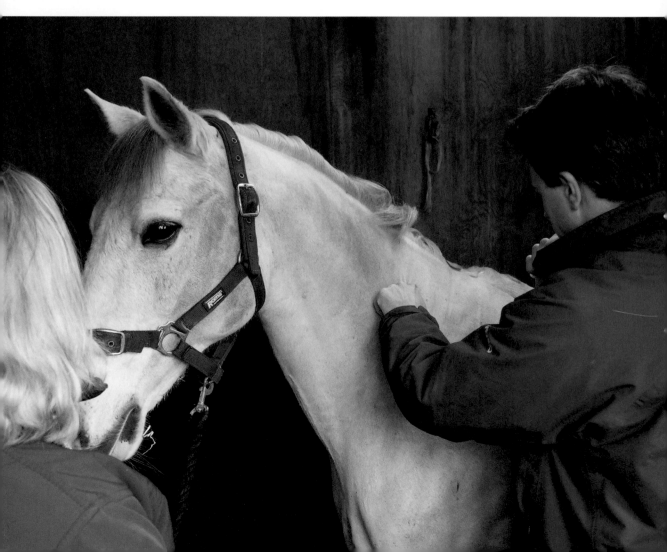

Ringworm

Ringworm is a contagious fungal infection of the skin which can also be passed on to humans. If undetected it will spread rapidly throughout a yard. It is therefore vital to recognise the symptoms.

Symptoms

Often circular, but not always, raised patches of hair appear on the coat. It can occur anywhere on the head or body but is commonly found in areas that come into contact with tack. The hair will eventually fall off, leaving a raw-looking sore. This will eventually dry out and the hair will grow back.

The vet records the pony's vaccination.

Treatment

◊ Isolate if possible.
◊ Call the vet to confirm the condition and oral or topical medication will then be prescribed.
◊ Do not groom, clip or ride as this will spread the infection.
◊ Do not let the horse come into contact with others or share equipment.

Prevention

◊ Young ponies are more at risk as they have less immunity.
◊ Thoroughly disinfect all equipment the infected horse has come into contact with. Ringworm spores can remain dormant on wooden surfaces for over a year, therefore it is highly important to disinfect the stable and trailer or horsebox.
◊ It is advisable to wear a specific set of clothing when dealing with the pony which is removed immediately after handling him.
◊ Avoid handling or stroking other ponies until yours is given the all clear.

Lice

Lice can affect any pony but are more commonly found in longer coats as they tend to go unnoticed and survive better.

Symptoms

The pony becomes very itchy and will rub their mane and tail. They will also bite their legs, leading to loss of hair and sore patches. Upon examination, the lice and eggs can be seen.

Causes

Older, neglected ponies or those with a weaker immune system are more susceptible. Lice spread through direct contact or the use of infected equipment and clothing, such as grooming kits and rugs.

Treatment

◊ It is possible to treat with a wash or powder but these are not always 100 per cent effective.
◊ It is more reliable to have the vet prescribe medication.

Prevention

◊ Isolate infected ponies until treatment is complete.
◊ Disinfect all contaminated equipment and clothing.

Mud fever

Mud fever is a skin condition that affects the lower limbs. It starts as a mild irritation that can develop into painful sores and become infected if not treated.

Symptoms

Crusty scabs usually develop at the back of the heels, often unnoticed if the pony has lots of feathers. When grooming, it will be possible to feel the scabs and see a yellow discharge. Eventually the hair will fall off leaving raw, inflamed skin. The legs will be hot, possibly swollen, and very sore to touch or flex. Lameness can also occur. The condition can quickly spread higher up the legs.

Causes

It is caused by a bacterium found in the soil. In wet, muddy conditions the skin on the legs becomes soft, allowing the bacteria to enter. Ponies with white legs and pink skin are more susceptible. Mud fever does not only affect ponies standing in wet, muddy fields, it can also occur when legs are frequently washed and not dried off with a towel.

Treatment

The pony should be brought in from the muddy field and stabled until the treatment has worked. If noticed early enough, it should not be necessary to call the vet but an experienced person may need to assist. Trim the hair around the affected area. The scabs need to be removed using hot water and an antiseptic, such as Hibiscrub. Poulticing may be required to soften more stubborn scabs. The legs should then be dried by gentle patting and not rubbed vigorously. Mud fever cream should then be applied. When possible, avoid dressing the wounds as fresh air will aid the healing. It may be necessary to cover deeper cracks to avoid the risk of infection. Keep the legs dry and the pony gently exercised to aid circulation. If the symptoms persist it will be necessary to call the vet.

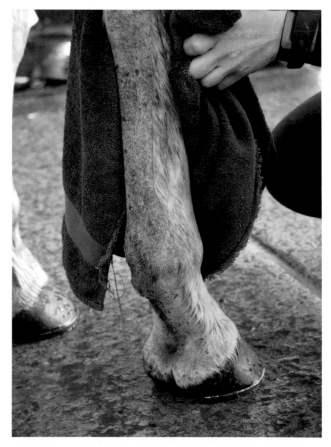

Towel drying white legs.

Prevention

◊ Avoid allowing the pony to stand in deep mud. It may be necessary at times to fence these areas off.
◊ Always thoroughly dry legs after washing.
◊ Protective boots or barrier cream can be applied to ponies that are susceptible to the condition. Thoroughly check the legs daily as the condition is more manageable if detected early.

Thrush

Thrush is an unpleasant infection that affects the pony's frog.

Symptoms

The frog produces a foul smell and sometimes black discharge. This will be noticed when picking out the hooves. The pony can show sensitivity in the area and, in severe cases, lameness.

Causes

It affects stabled ponies more often, especially when standing in wet, dirty bedding. Failing to pick out the feet on a daily basis and irregular visits from the farrier are also major causes.

Treatment

The feet should be thoroughly picked out and scrubbed with an iodine solution. This must be carried out for a number of days. The foot should then be allowed to dry and an antiseptic spray applied. Bedding must be clean and dry if treatment is to be successful.

Prevention

◊ Pick out feet daily, before and after exercise, scrub at least once a week.
◊ Keep bedding as dry and clean as possible.

*Scrubbing the foot
to prevent thrush.*

◊   Regular visits from the farrier to trim and dress the feet.
◊   Avoid the pony standing in wet, muddy conditions.

Cushing's disease

Cushing's disease is fairly common in older ponies and it is important to recognise the symptoms in order to manage the condition. It can affect all breeds and types, but is more commonly found in ponies over the age of fifteen.

Causes

It is a progressive disorder that causes the pituitary gland to dysfunction. Over time, small tumours can develop on the gland which unbalances hormone levels, creating the symptoms we see.

Symptoms

◊   Weight loss. The pony may develop a 'pot belly' and lose muscle on his neck and hindquarters.

143

◊ More prone to laminitis.
◊ Excessive thirst and urination.
◊ Pony becomes run down and lethargic.
◊ Prone to infection.
◊ Mouth ulcers.
◊ Grows a long thick coat all year round.

Treatment

If suspected, the vet will need to run a blood test to confirm the condition. It cannot be cured, but daily medication can improve the pony's quality of life and is not too expensive. Extra care must be taken in caring for the pony to prevent secondary problems.

Secondary problems

- Reduce the risk of laminitis by strict control of grazing.
- Regular dental care to reduce the risk of infection in the mouth.
- Manage the diet to control weight loss.
- Diligent wound management to reduce the risk of further infection.
- Keep vaccinations and worming up to date.
- Regularly check for lice.
- Clip the pony, if he sweats a great deal, to make him more comfortable.

Sweet itch

A condition that causes the pony to become itchy, usually around the mane and tail region.

Causes

An allergic reaction from being bitten by a certain type of midge.

Symptoms

The symptoms usually occur during spring, summer and early autumn, disappearing during the winter months. The pony will be seen scratching himself along his mane line, tail and, in severe cases, other areas of his body and legs. Bald patches will occur and often develop into broken skin and open sores.

Treatment and prevention

Keep the area clean by using soothing shampoos. Sweet itch lotion should be applied several times a day. This can be purchased over the counter. Rugs specially designed to protect the pony can be worn in the stable and field. Avoid turning out at dawn and dusk when the midges are at their worst, and try not to stable the pony close to the muck heap. If symptoms persist, the vet may suggest a steroid injection to alleviate the problem.

Fly sheet to help prevent sweet itch.

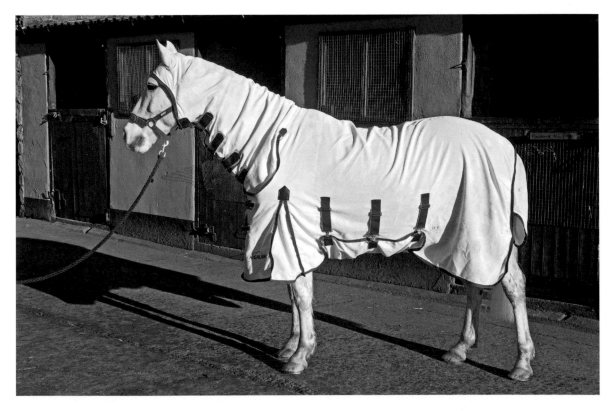

Allergies

Causes

An allergic reaction is commonly caused by the pony reacting to something he has eaten. If he has been in the field, it is likely a plant or weed, often found in hedgerows. It can also be caused by a change in feed or bedding. As with humans, they can also react to an insect sting or bite. Medication given orally or topically can also be a cause.

Symptoms

Allergies can appear in the form of small lumps and bumps or much larger swellings on the skin. In severe cases they can affect the eyes, mouth, nose and rectum. The skin may feel hot and the pony may be itchy and restless. In other cases they may cause no discomfort.

Treatment

When possible, identify and remove the cause. Mild reactions usually do not require treatment and will disappear in a day or two. If the pony is showing signs of distress or the mucous membranes are affected, the vet should be called immediately. Otherwise, try to keep the skin cool, avoid exercise and too much clothing. If symptoms have not improved after forty-eight hours, the vet should be called.

Prevention

Regularly check around the field for weeds and poisonous plants. Once the cause is identified, remove and avoid future contact when possible.

Routine worming

All ponies must follow a routine worming programme otherwise they are at risk of serious health issues such as colic, loss of condition, a dull coat and lethargy.

Worming the pony.

If your pony is at livery, it is likely the yard will have a worming programme that you join. They will often insist the pony is wormed on arrival and not turned out for two days after treatment. Others may require you to have a worm count done by the vet.

If you are using your own programme, ask for your instructor's advice. There are several wormers on the market to choose from. Wormers come with detailed instructions. It is advisable to have someone show you how to administer it for the first time as it is often not as easy as it looks. Ponies who are not keen can be very quick to recognise what is coming and make the task difficult, often wasting the wormer.

Teeth

Your pony should have his teeth checked by the vet or an equine dentist every six months. Due to the action of the jaw when chewing, sharp

A horse having routine dentistry.

Time to call the dentist

- Routine visits.
- Pony stops or shows difficulty eating.
- Quidding – this is when food is dropped out of the mouth and balls of chewed food may be found in the stable.
- Pony becomes head shy and difficult when applying the bridle.
- Pony is more sensitive in the mouth when ridden, throwing his head up or being difficult to turn.
- Foul breath.

edges occur on the molars. If these are not rasped down, they can interfere with the gums, causing painful lesions inside the mouth. Older ponies may suffer from tooth decay, tooth loss or need some teeth removing.

Vaccinations

It is essential that your pony is covered for tetanus. It may be a requirement by the livery yard that he is also covered for equine influenza. The two can be given as a combined injection. If, when you buy your pony, he doesn't come with either of these, it is essential that you contact the vet to get the procedure started as soon as possible.

First aid kit

It is advisable that you own a basic first aid kit that is kept close to the pony and can also be taken to competitions.

Important numbers

The following phone numbers should be kept somewhere close to your pony in case of an emergency.

- Veterinarian
- Farrier
- Dentist
- Feed store

First aid kit

- **Vetwrap x 2**
- **Stable bandages × 4**
- **Gamgee**
- **Dry dressing**
- **Animalintex poultice**
- **Cotton wool**
- **Hibiscrub**
- **Antiseptic cream or gel**
- **Tetcin spray**
- **Disinfectant**
- **Epsom salts**
- **Vaseline**
- **Sun screen**
- **Fly repellent**
- **Thermometer**
- **Scissors**
- **Sterile bowl**
- **Towels**
- **Tape.**

- Bedding and hay supplier

- Saddler

- Instructor

- Insurance company and policy number.

Records

It is essential to keep records of information relating to your pony's care, health and well-being.

Health records

These should include worming, vaccinations and dentist. Any health issues or lameness should be recorded, no matter how minor. This information may be useful if the vet needs to be called for a more serious matter. Keep a file and add to it when necessary. It is important to have a system to remind you when worming, vaccinations and the dentist are due. Remember to allow enough time for treatment to be arranged or purchased. This is especially important for the vaccinations. If the due date is missed, the course has to be started again, which will prove very costly.

11
Shoeing

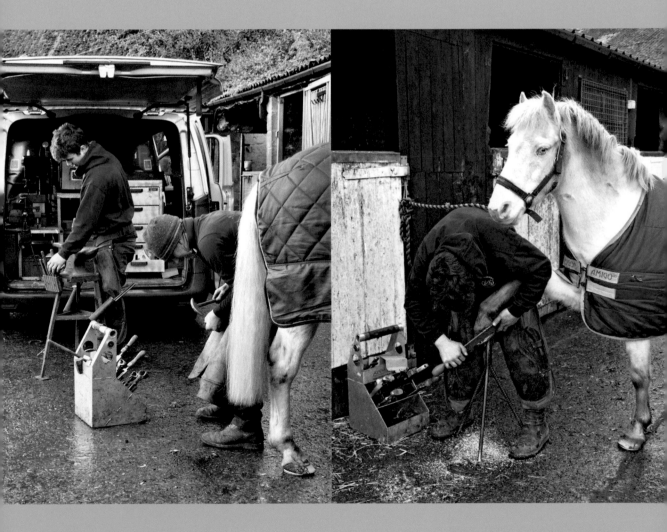

Care

of the pony's feet is of utmost importance if you are going to avoid problems. Feet are often neglected in an attempt to reduce costs, as farrier visits are one of the biggest expenses involved in owning a pony. However, this tends to lead to more expense when problems arise. It is the owner's responsibility to keep the foot clean and healthy on a daily basis and to recognise when the pony needs to be seen by the farrier. Most ponies will require a visit every five to eight weeks. Foot growth is slower in winter so they can usually last a week or so longer between visits at this time of year.

A visit from the farrier.

When to call the farrier

- Lost, loose or twisted shoe

- Foot too long and needs trimming

- Foot overgrowing the shoe

- Risen clenches

- Possible lameness in the foot

- Sudden tripping and stumbling

- Following laminitis.

Left: Toe too long.

Above: Risen clenches.

Where to find a farrier

If you are keeping your pony at livery, find out from the manager what the farrier policy is. They may use one who visits the yard on a regular basis and shoes all the horses, if possible your pony can be added to the list. This system works well as the farrier is at the yard regularly and available to deal with emergencies.

If you have to organise your own, ask locally who others use, what reputation they have and how much they charge. The qualities to look for are reliable, patient and calm with the horses. You need to ask if the farrier has a colleague that you can use if they are sick or on holiday. It is important that he regards your pony as highly as he would a top competition horse. If the shoeing is done badly, problems will occur in no time.

Shod or barefoot

Often, ponies in light work do not require shoes or will just need to be shod in front. Some yards will stipulate that hind shoes cannot be worn if the pony is to be turned out in company. The reason for

Hot shoeing.

this is that a shod pony is capable of causing serious injury if it kicks another. Ponies that have strong, well-balanced feet are likely to get away with being barefoot if they are worked on a decent surface. In general, black hooves are stronger than white and don't break up as much. A foot with plenty of heel will cope better than a flatter shaped hoof. Some ponies can quite happily do road work unshod, while others can work on grass or a soft surface but not on the hard.

If the pony is shod when he arrives it is advisable to keep him in shoes to begin with. Ask the farrier for their opinion of the feet in respect to balance, health and condition. If they suggest the pony has good feet, you might then raise the question of removing the hind shoes.

If the pony is barefoot, it is still essential the feet are cared for and not neglected by yourself and the farrier. The pony may become 'foot sore'. He will display this through lameness or becoming shorter in his stride. The feet may also feel warm. If the symptoms persist, it will be necessary to put him back in shoes.

If your pony has weak or brittle feet the farrier may suggest a supplement or a topical hoof conditioner. The latter is applied to the clean, dry hoof on a daily basis.

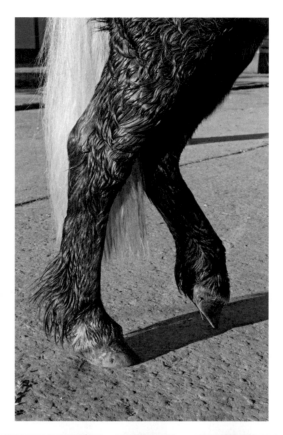

Left: Barefoot.

Below left: Brittle foot requiring hoof dressing.

Below: Applying hoof dressing.

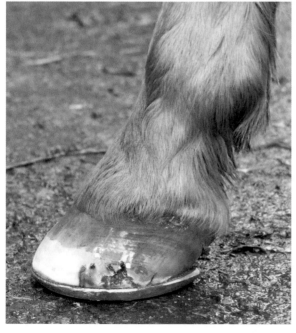

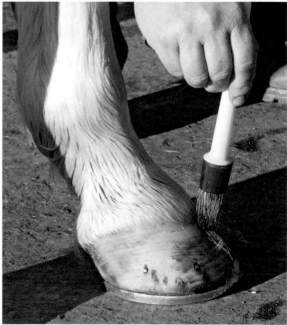

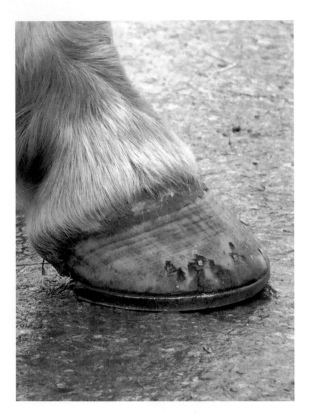

A well-shod foot.

Check after the farrier

When the pony has been shod it is important to check he is sound. Even the most experienced farrier can make a mistake. This is usually caused by a nail being put in too close to the white line, an area which is the union of the sensitive and insensitive parts of the hoof. The term nail bind is when the nail is touching but not penetrating the white line. This would probably feel like he is wearing a pair of shoes that are too tight. This problem can often right itself in a day or two. If the pony is severely lame, he is likely to have a nail prick, where the nail has gone into the sensitive part. This will need to be removed as an abscess may form. The farrier should be called back as soon as possible to deal with the problem.

Records

Keep records in your file of when your pony is shod and what the farrier has done. It is helpful if you book the next appointment when the farrier is there as they tend to get very busy. If you wait until the pony needs shoeing, it may be a couple of weeks before the farrier is available. This could result in the feet becoming overgrown and possibly lost shoes or lameness. Not only is this uncomfortable for the pony, it can also be frustrating and disappointing for your child, especially if they have competitions or Pony Club activities planned.

12
Tack and equipment

There are certain items of tack and equipment that are essential and others which are optional. The following chapter offers advice on buying, fitting and maintaining good condition of the tack.

Headcollar and rope

A pony is usually sold with a headcollar and rope. It is, however, advisable to buy one as there is no guarantee what condition it will be in or how well it will fit. It is not an expensive piece of equipment and it is handy to have a spare.

It is essential to buy the correct size of headcollar as an ill-fitting one can either cause rubs if it is too tight or come off if too loose.

Headcollar size guide	
Foal	Foal
Mini	Miniature ponies
Shetland	10.2hh to 12.2hh
Pony	12.2hh to 14hh
Cob	14hh to 15.2hh
Full	15.2hh to 17hh
X full	17hh +

This chart is only a rough guide as the breed of the pony will have an impact on the size of its head; native breeds tend to be on the larger side more so than Thoroughbred types. Different makes will vary in size and it is worth asking if they tend to be a small or large fit.

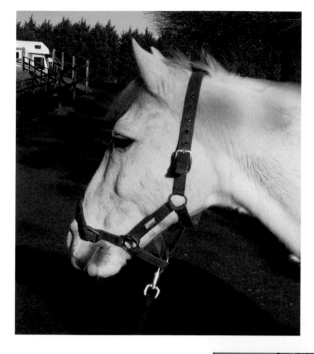

Headcollars vary in design and come in different colours and materials. Leather is smarter, more expensive to buy and needs to be cleaned on a regular basis. For this reason, they are usually used for competition. The nylon headcollar is more common for everyday use. They can be very simple and inexpensive or come with extra padding and cost more. It is useful if the headcollar has two fastenings, making it easier to put on and off.

Above left: Headcollar is too loose.

Above: A headcollar fitted correctly.

Left: A headcollar with two fastenings.

Bridle

If your pony has come with a bridle, it is advisable to have your instructor check the condition and fit. It is essential that the stitching is in good order and the leather is not dry and brittle, predisposing it to snapping. If the pony did not come with a bridle, make note of what bit and noseband he was wearing, and if your instructor thinks that the equipment is suitable, it is safest to go with the same arrangement.

The make and quality of the leather will influence the price. Fashionable brands can be expensive but are, more often than not, good quality. It is possible to go for a lesser known brand which will still be suitable. English leather is usually a better choice than less expensive leather that has been imported.

Bridle size guide	
Small pony	Up to 12.2hh
Pony	12.2hh to 14hh
Cob	14hh to 15.2hh
Full	15.2hh +

Noseband

The simplest noseband is the cavesson. This has no real purpose other than improving the appearance of the bridle. If the pony goes nicely in this then there is no reason to go for anything more complicated.

If the pony has a tendency to get strong when ridden, then he may benefit from wearing a noseband that will help keep the mouth closed and prevent him crossing his jaws and evading the bit. There are three common choices, the flash, drop or grackle. Putting on a slightly stronger noseband can often be a better solution than changing the bit.

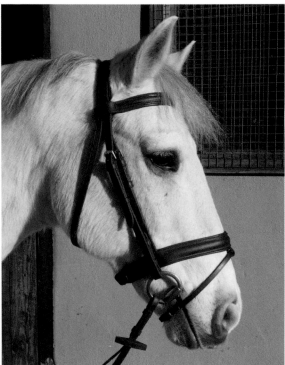

Reins

It is important that the bridle has the correct length of reins. If too short, the child may end up tipping forward; if too long, they can get caught up in the stirrups. Often children are expected to ride with a rein that is too thick.

A thinner rein is easier on the fingers and more comfortable. If one side of the rein is covered in rubber, it will prevent the reins slipping from the child's hands.

Above left: A cavesson noseband.

Above right: A flash noseband.

Left: A grackle noseband.

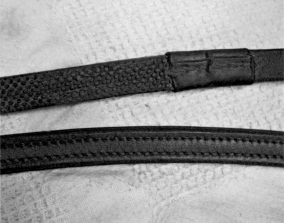

Clockwise from above: A rein that is too thick.

Reins with rubber on one side.

A knot is tied in the reins.

Reins that are too long.

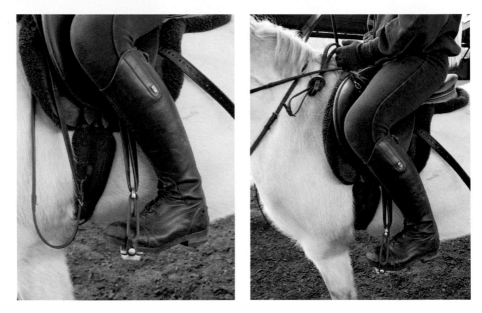

Bit

Ideally the pony will be ridden in a snaffle. This is the most common and simplest bit. There are many variations on the snaffle and advice from your instructor should be sought to help you choose the correct one. It is also essential that the bit is the correct size and shape for the pony's mouth. If he is not comfortable with his bit, he is not going to be very happy when ridden.

Sometimes it is possible to go to a 'bit bank'. This allows you to try a bit before you purchase. This should be considered if you are in doubt of what to choose.

Above left: A selection of snaffle bits.

Above right: A selection of stronger bits.

Fitting the bridle

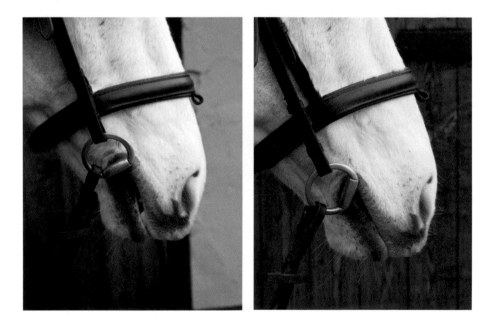

Far left: Bit too high.

Left: Bit too low.

Your instructor should help you fit the bridle. Here are a few guidelines to help you:

- The bridle should slip easily over the ears.

- The bit should sit comfortably in the corners of the mouth, showing two to three wrinkles.

- The throatlatch should be fastened allowing a few fingers between the cheek and the strap.

- The cavesson noseband lies flat, allowing two fingers between the noseband and the front of the nose.

-

Fitting the throatlatch.

Saddle

Fitting a saddle is a much more complex procedure than that of other tack and equipment, therefore it is advisable to seek help from a professional. The best way to do this is by arranging for a saddle fitter to bring a selection of saddles to your yard. They can be tried on the pony and your child is allowed to ride in them. If possible, your instructor should also be present as they will be a better judge on how suitable the saddle is for your child.

Type of saddle

There are different types of saddles designed to help both horse and rider achieve the best result in various disciplines. The specific design helps a rider's position, balance and safety. The most commonly used saddles are the dressage, jumping, showing and general purpose, the latter is often referred to as the GP. It is not necessary to go for a specialist saddle unless competing at a

Above: An experienced saddle fitter.

Left: Checking the fit of the saddle.

165

Above: A jumping saddle.

Right: A general purpose saddle.

more serious level. The GP saddle is designed to enable the rider to ride with a varied length of stirrup to suit both flat work and jumping. Until riding at a higher level, a child does not tend to alter the stirrup length more than a hole or two. The GP is often a more comfortable saddle for both horse and rider.

Many saddlers will deal in second-hand pony saddles which frequently come up for sale as children grow out of them quickly. This is a cheaper option than buying new and serves the purpose just as well. When choosing a saddler, find someone who comes with a good reputation.

Ill-fitting saddles

A poorly fitting saddle will very quickly have an impact on how your pony behaves when ridden. It is advisable to know how to check that your pony is not sore and the signs he may show if uncomfortable when ridden.

When grooming, note if the pony is sensitive on his back or girth area. Frequently run a hand over these areas to check for lumps, swellings or sensitivity. He will display this by putting his ears back, swishing his tail and even threatening to bite or kick. Take note of his coat growth in

these areas and whether it looks like it has been rubbed or if there are any bald patches. White hairs may be seen at the withers, this indicates that at some point the pony has had a poorly fitting saddle or rug causing a sore on the skin. Eventually, when this heals the hair can grow back white.

Above left: Checking the back for sores.

Above right: White hairs showing an old saddle injury.

When ridden, the pony may show the following behaviours if the saddle is not comfortable.

- Reluctant to go forward.

- Moves with a shorter stride than usual.

- More forward than normal and rushing.

- Ears back and tail swishing.

- Bucking.

- Napping.

Your pony may change shape as he gains or loses weight and muscle. This can often affect the fit of the saddle. Your instructor should keep an eye on this and advise you on what action to take. It may not be necessary to change the saddle as there are many types of numnahs and pads available that can help.

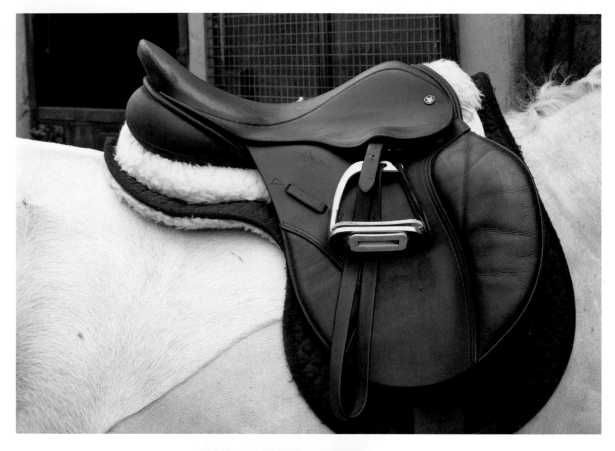

Above: A pad to correct the fit of the saddle.

Right: A selection of girths.

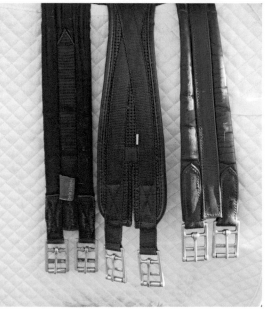

Girths

When choosing a girth it is advisable to buy one that is easy to clean. The size of the girth should allow for the pony to lose or gain a few kilos which he will undoubtedly do throughout the year.

Stirrup irons and leathers

Leathers must be in good condition. It is essential to check the stitching when buying second hand. The irons must be a suitable size for your child. If they are too big, the foot often slips out or through the stirrup; if too small, there is a danger of the foot getting stuck. Safety stirrups are advisable for children.

Far left: Stirrup iron too small.

Left: Safety stirrup.

Neck strap

Neck straps are a MUST for all children. Many people view a neck strap as an aid for a beginner rider and can't wait to get rid of it. It is, however, useful at any level and many top riders use them in both training and competition.

The child can use the neck strap to aid their balance, rather than pulling on the pony's mouth. It can also help to keep the hands low when learning to canter and jump. The neck strap will help with security if the pony is a little fresh and pops in a buck or spooks. An old stirrup leather is often used. This can be a little bulky for small hands and a martingale neck strap is more suitable.

Martingale

There are two types of martingale used, running and standing, the former being the more common. The purpose of the martingale is to prevent the pony raising his head beyond the angle of control. As mentioned before, this is not a trail you would expect to see from a first pony. A martingale is often used regardless of how the pony goes and can usually be removed without affecting his way of going. Your instructor should advise you if they feel the pony would benefit from wearing one.

Running martingale.

Crupper

A crupper is used to help stop a saddle from slipping up the pony's neck. This often happens on smaller, fat ponies that have very little wither.

Boots

The purpose of a boot is to prevent injury to the legs. There are many different types of boot available. Some of the most commonly used and relevant to your needs are listed below.

Brushing boots

This boot protects the lower leg when riding and lungeing. Brushing is a term used when the pony knocks one leg against the other, causing injury on the inside of the leg. A brushing boot will give protection against this, and also protect the leg when jumping if the pony hits a pole.

Left: Poorly fitting boots.

Middle: Hind fetlock boots.

Right: Front tendon boots.

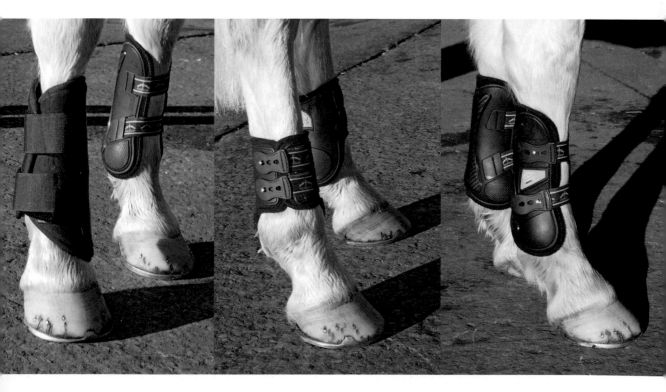

Overreach boots.

Overreach boots

An overreach is caused by a hind foot treading on the heel of the front foot. This is more common when galloping and jumping or when the pony is turned out in the field. If your pony is prone to this or has a tendency to lose front shoes, overreach boots may be helpful.

Travel boots

These are worn to give the pony protection when travelling. They cover a large area of the legs and are much easier to apply than bandages.

Fitting boots

All types of boots will need to be fitted correctly otherwise they can actually cause injury. Your instructor should advise you if they feel your pony should wear them.

Rugs

There are many types of rugs used for different purposes. The main reason is to keep the pony warm, dry and clean.

Stable rugs

Stable rugs are worn indoors, mainly during the winter. They come in various weights (thicknesses): light, medium and heavy. An unclipped native breed would usually require a lightweight rug, whereas a clipped-out Thoroughbred will need a heavyweight one.

Stable rug.

New Zealand rugs

New Zealand rugs are waterproof and designed for outdoor use but can also be used as a stable rug. Like stable rugs, they come in various weights. Some also have a neck cover which is useful to keep the pony clean, as well as offering extra protection.

Coolers

Coolers are used after exercise or when travelling. They are breathable which allows the pony to dry after hard work or a bath.

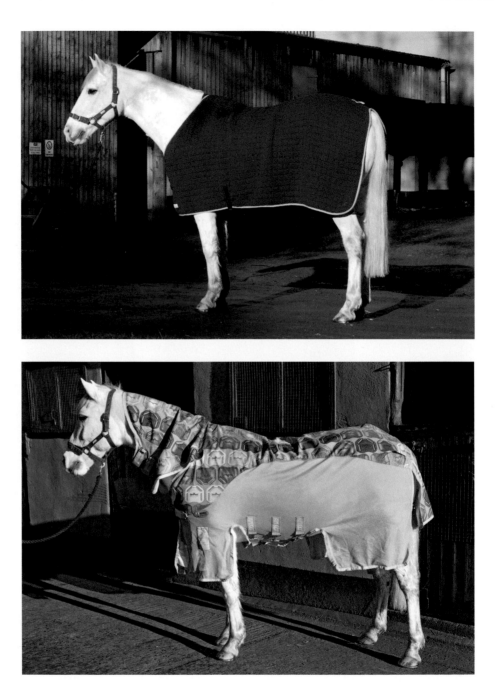

Above: Cooler.

Right: Fly sheet.

Fly sheets

Fly sheets are useful in summer to protect the pony from irritating flies. They can also be used if the pony is prone to rubbing his mane and tail.

Fitting rugs

It is essential that rugs are fitted well, otherwise they will quickly rub and cause the pony to develop sores. These are commonly found on the withers and shoulders. The pony should be measured by following a straight line from the centre of his chest along his belly to the point of the buttock. The chart below gives a guide to what size rug you will require.

Rug sizing according to height			
Hands (hh)	Feet (ft) inches	Hands (hh)	Feet (ft) inches
11.2hh	4ft	13.2hh	5ft
12hh	4ft 3	14hh	5ft 3
12.2hh	4ft 6	14.2hh	5ft 6
13hh	4ft 9		

This is just a guide. As well as being the correct length, the rug must also be the correct depth and fit well around the pony's shoulders and withers.

Rug is poorly fitted and slipped down over the pony's shoulders.

Tail bandage.

Tail bandage

A tail bandage should be worn for travelling to protect the tail if the pony has a tendency to rub. It can also be used after grooming or before a competition to improve the appearance of the tail. It is essential to be shown how to correctly and safely apply the bandage as, if it is too tight, permanent damage can be done. It should not be left on for long periods of time and never overnight.

Tack cleaning

Tack cleaning is an essential part of stable management and should be done on a regular basis. This will ensure the leather is kept clean and supple, making it easier to work with, and will improve its appearance. It also gives you a chance to thoroughly check over the stitching and buckles for safety purposes.

Procedure

Ideally your tack should have a general clean after use and more thoroughly once a week. The difference being that the saddle and bridle are 'stripped' or taken apart for the thorough clean. This enables you to check its condition in more detail and clean the buckle areas.

Equipment

- **Leather oil/dressing**
- **Saddle soap**
- **Sponges**
- **Towel**
- **Brasso/metal polish.**

When riding, the leather that comes into contact with the pony's skin and coat will become covered in grease. It will also become muddy and wet during the winter months causing it to dry out if not cleaned and treated.

Bridle and martingale

The bit should be cleaned by placing it in hot water. If the bridle is taken apart, the bit can be soaked in a bowl or bucket. The hotter the water, the more effective it is at removing the grease. Soak a clean sponge in the hot water and thoroughly squeeze it out. The leather should not become too wet as this will dry it out even more. Remove all the mud and grease from the leather. Once this is done, use a separate damp sponge to apply the saddle soap. This

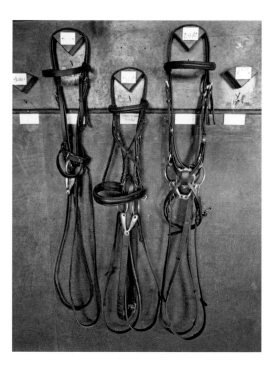

Bridles tied up neatly after cleaning.

should not appear foamy on the leather. If it does, too much water is being applied. While cleaning, check all the stitching is in good order. If the bridle has been taken apart, it is important that it goes back together correctly with the buckles fastened on the right holes. Once complete, the reins can be tied up in the throatlatch and hung neatly.

Saddle

The girth and numnah should be removed from the saddle after riding. It is handy to have a couple of each to enable them to be washed and dried on a regular basis. Avoid using wet or damp girths and numnahs as this may cause girth galls or saddle sores. Dirty material can also cause problems on the skin.

During cleaning, the stirrups and girth should be removed. The stirrup irons can then be soaked in hot water. As with the bridle, the saddle and leathers should be wiped over with hot water and then saddle soap applied. Special attention should be paid to the stitching on the girth straps and stirrup leathers. Applying too much soap to the seat of the saddle and saddle flaps can cause staining to jodhpurs. If the girth is leather it can be cleaned in the same way. A saddle cover is useful to keep the saddle clean and protect it from scratches. This is particularly useful when travelling.

Oils/conditioners

Oils and conditioners can be used to treat new saddlery or tack that has become very stiff due to a good soaking or neglect. The leather should be wiped over with a damp sponge to remove grease, mud or mould. It should then be towel dried before the product is applied. Finally, the tack should be placed in a warm environment to encourage the oil or conditioner to soak into the leather. This will not happen if it is left in a cold room.

Metal

The appearance of any metal work on your tack will be improved by cleaning it with metal polish. This is highly recommended prior to competition, especially if competing in a tack and turnout class.

When possible, all tack should be stored in warm, dry conditions. If your tack is not going to be in use for a period of time, it can be stored. This will help prevent it becoming mouldy. The leather should be cleaned and treated with oil or a conditioner. It can then be wrapped in newspaper and stored in a warm, dry room. Any needed repairs should be done before the tack goes into storage.

13
Exercise

Ensuring your pony receives some form of exercise on a regular basis is essential to his well-being. The amount and type of exercise provided will depend on many factors. This chapter will give you help and ideas on keeping your pony healthy and happy in his work.

Amount of exercise required

Ponies are generally very resilient and, unlike horses, do not require a fitness and exercise programme until they are competing at a high level. Most cope with being ridden at the weekends and left through the week when time does not permit. An unfit pony is not likely to sustain the same injuries as would an unfit horse. Therefore, we do not need to have our ponies very fit unless we are preparing for an event such as Pony Club camp or a day's hunting. It would be unfair to drag your pony from the field and ask him to do this.

The amount of exercise a pony requires will be governed by several factors.

Living out

If the pony lives out full time he will exercise himself sufficiently to aid his circulation and keep everything moving. It will usually also prevent him from becoming too fresh when ridden. He is, however, unlikely to exert himself very often. So unless he is receiving other forms of exercise, his fitness level will not increase and he will be at risk of gaining weight, especially in the spring and summer.

Ideally, the grass kept pony will be ridden at weekends. This will be sufficient to keep him ticking over or in 'light work'. It is essential to keep an eye on his weight. If he starts to gain weight then grazing must be reduced or more exercise introduced.

Stabled

A pony that is stabled full time, or partly, will require more exercise to prevent him becoming fresh or bored. If he is older, his joints will suffer from little movement which may result in stiffness or possible lameness. Ideally, he will spend some time out in the paddock. If this is reduced or not possible in the winter months, then other forms of exercise must be introduced on a daily basis. Unless injured, a pony will not benefit from standing in the stable for long periods of time.

Forms of exercise

Ridden

Bigger ponies of 13.2hh to 14.2hh can be ridden by a small adult. There may be someone local or at your livery yard who is able to exercise him when your child cannot. If competent, the adult rider can also school the pony, making him an easier ride for your child.

Below left: An adult schooling a pony.

Below right: Using the horse walker for exercise.

Horse walker

Most larger yards have a horse walker. This can be used to exercise the pony if other options are not available. Overuse should be avoided as working on a tight circle can cause soundness issues if done frequently or for long periods of time. It is also a rather monotonous form of exercise.

Lungeing

Tacked up for lungeing.

This form of exercise is beneficial for fitness and can improve the pony's way of going, making him easier for your child to ride. If you plan to lunge the pony yourself, it is advisable to get assistance with learning how to do this correctly and safely. It is not ideal to lunge every day as it involves

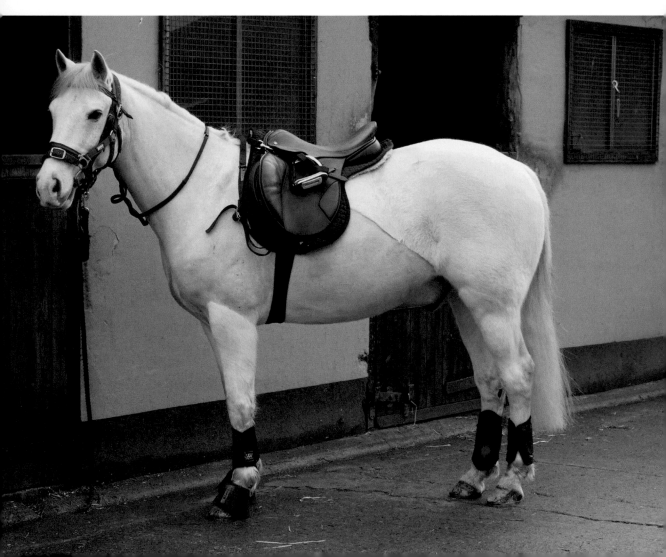

the pony working on a smallish circle, which does put a certain amount of strain on the legs. Lungeing for twenty to thirty minutes, three to four times per week, is acceptable. To prevent injury, lungeing must be done on a suitable surface, ideally in an enclosed arena. If it is necessary to lunge in a field, care must be taken when the ground is wet as the pony may slip. It is not advisable to lunge on hard ground during the summer months.

Above: Lungeing with side reins to improve the pony's way of going.

Left: Lungeing for exercise.

Ride and lead.

Hand walking

If a horse walker is not available to you, then hand walking smaller, well-mannered ponies is an option. It is also a great way to get yourself fit. It is advisable to use a bridle, especially if you are going on any roads. Even the smallest ponies can get very strong if they decide to go!

Ride and lead

This is an ideal way to give the pony a decent amount of exercise. The pony is led from a ridden horse. This should only be done by a competent rider and both ridden and led pony must be well mannered and good in traffic. It is advisable to try this in the arena first before going out for a hack.

Fitness

An average child's pony does not need to be too fit and is usually best kept in 'maintenance or light work'. This requires twenty minutes to one hour of work, three to four times per week. Doing more than this will gradually increase the pony's fitness. Getting the pony 'too fit' can cause behavioural problems. If the work is suddenly dropped and the pony does not feel he is getting enough exercise he may become unruly. A common mistake is to give a fresh pony more work, consequently increasing his fitness levels.

If you are intending to hunt the pony, then he will need to be fitter. The work should be increased to forty to sixty minutes, four to five times per week, and ideally include more cantering and some hill work if possible. As the pony gets fitter, he may become more of a handful but it is presumed that a child who is ready to go hunting will be capable of coping with this. If you are planning on taking your child to the children's meet on a lead rein, then there is no need to change his work regime as he will be required to do very little.

Ponies tend to be ridden more during school holidays, thereby increasing their fitness level. Pony Club camp usually takes place during the summer holidays, so hopefully your pony will have a few weeks to prepare. If camp falls at the beginning of the holidays, it is necessary to increase the pony's work before this to ensure his well-being.

Children hunting.

Above: Younger children benefit from group lessons.

Right: Older children benefit more from private lessons.

Lessons

If your child and pony are going to progress together it is advisable to continue having lessons. This can be privately arranged or done through an organisation such as Pony Club or Riding Club. Younger children tend to become easily distracted or bored on a one-to-one basis and get much more enjoyment from riding in a group. As your child gets older they may show interest in attending local shows and competitions. They will then need more help with the technical aspects of riding their pony. Private lessons can be more beneficial for this.

Pony Club

Joining the local Pony Club branch is a great way to improve your child's riding and stable management skills, and gives them the opportunity to socialise with other children and participate in mounted and unmounted rallies (lessons) and camp. Membership is open to anyone up to the age of twenty-five.

Your local Pony Club will offer your child education on riding and pony care, as well as the opportunity to make new friends.

'*I had the most amazing childhood during my Pony Club days and if I could give half of my experience to my children they will be very lucky. It is amazing for building confidence, being responsible, having to make decisions and commitments whatever the situation, dealing with highs and lows, making friends, interacting with strangers, having lots of fun, learning to control nerves, being given lots of opportunities, being part of lots of different teams as well as being an individual. Competing equally with the opposite sex (apart from tetrathlon) at the same time having to have the connection with an animal (I believe one if not the only sport this happens in). Opportunity to work towards badges, test all the way through the ages. When I took my A Test it was such an honour and achievement to gain that it opens doors not just for first-time happy hackers [but] also for the older children.'*

Georgie

Pony Club also offers various badges and tests to work towards, ranging from mini achievement badges for those just starting out, up to the prestigious 'A Test', which is the highest test in Pony Club. It is recognised worldwide as a top achievement, as well as a qualification for someone wanting a career with horses. Many top international riders started their careers at Pony Club.

As your child develops, they may also be interested in competing for Pony Club teams. This could be:

- Dressage
- Endurance riding
- Eventing
- Mounted games
- Polo
- Polocrosse
- Show jumping
- Tetrathlon
- Racing (recently introduced).

Your branch will also hold various events throughout the year, ranging from educational visits, trips to top shows and competitions, quizzes and other inter-branch events.

Above left: Children having fun at Pony Club.

Above right: Children doing Pony Club achievement badges.

Left: A Pony Club dressage test.

Riding Clubs

Riding Clubs offer a range of events and training for amateur riders. It is more suited to older children and adults, although some Riding Clubs accommodate junior membership and offer activities more specific to younger riders.

Competitions

As your child progresses, they will probably show an interest in taking part in some sort of competition, more so if they have been attending Pony Club activities. There are numerous little shows and competitions suitable for getting your child started, especially during the summer months. If possible try to attend several shows as a spectator, this will enable you to see what classes there are and the performance requirements for the different disciplines. It also gives you a chance to note the dress code and how horses and ponies are 'turned out' and presented for competition.

Far left: A child waiting to compete.

Left: A pony race.

Before going to a show, it is advisable to discuss with your instructor if they think your child is ready for the experience and what classes would be suitable to enter. Hopefully, your pony will have had prior experience and know how to behave in this environment. Your child should have attended group lessons or Pony Club rallies so they are familiar and confident when riding in company. Often at competitions, there are lots of ponies and children who are out of control and therefore not ready to be there. Your child needs to have sufficient control over their own pony to be able to avoid an unsafe situation. Many local shows offer lead rein classes. This is an ideal way to introduce a small child to competition.

Having fun at a Christmas show.

14
Clipping and turnout

At some stage, it is likely that your pony will require clipping. This chapter covers the reasons for clipping, types and suitability of clip, clipping procedure and care of the clipped pony. It will also cover turnout, explaining how to make your pony look presentable through trimming and plaiting.

Clipping

Reasons for clipping

In winter time, your pony will undoubtedly grow a thicker coat. How thick this is will depend on several factors. Native breeds and cob types will grow a much heavier coat than a finer breed such as a Thoroughbred or Arab. They do, however, moult in the spring and develop a finer summer coat. This changes with all types of ponies as they get older; the coat grows much thicker and the pony tends to hang on to it, even during the warmer months. As mentioned earlier, a pony with Cushing's disease will grow a heavier coat. Ponies living out without rugs will adapt to the cold weather in the winter months and have a thicker coat than one living in and wearing rugs.

Ponies with heavy coats will sweat more when exercised. Excess sweating can lead to a loss of condition. Your pony should not be rugged up until he is cool and dry, otherwise he may continue to sweat under the rug, causing him discomfort. A wet pony left without a rug on to dry will quickly get chilly in cold weather. It can be time consuming waiting to change the rug from a cooler to his stable rug or New Zealand. Heavy coats are harder to keep clean and healthy and therefore more likely to contract bacterial or fungal infections. The thick hair can hide such conditions, along with lumps, bumps and cuts. If problems with the skin are not detected early, they are more likely to develop into something more serious.

Grooming the unclipped pony is much harder work, especially when he comes in from the field covered in mud. Daylight hours are often

A pony with a full winter coat.

precious during the winter months and less time spent grooming means more time available for riding.

A shaggy pony can often look very untidy. Giving him a clip will improve his appearance, which is important when attending Pony Club rallies and competitions.

When to clip

You will start to notice a change in your pony's coat between September and October. This will continue to grow thicker until January or February time. The growth rate will then slow down and he will hang onto his coat until the warmer spring weather arrives.

Generally horses and ponies are clipped from mid-September through to February. Up to Christmas they may require a clip as often as every two weeks if in hard work such as hunting. However, most ponies would not require this and one clip before Christmas and one after would be quite sufficient.

Horses and ponies that are destined for the show ring are given the last clip no later than the end of February to avoid interfering with growth of the summer coat. It may be necessary to clip all year round if you have an old pony or one suffering from Cushing's disease.

Types of clip

The amount of hair you remove will depend on several factors.

- How thick the coat is and how much the pony sweats.

- The amount and type of work he is in.

- If the pony is living in or out.

- Temperament of the pony – clipping can result in the pony's behaviour being much sharper and he may become naughty when ridden.

- Condition of the pony – an older pony may be more difficult to keep weight on and feel the cold much more.

- Health issues.

- Appearance.

The following sections will discuss the more common types of clip. The type of clip you choose may depend on how your pony responds to being clipped. It is wise to start by removing a small amount of hair and seeing how the pony reacts to this, more can always be removed at a later stage.

Neck and belly

This is a very common clip given to ponies. It removes some of the hair from the neck, where the pony tends to sweat the most. It can be taken under the belly, which helps when removing mud from this area.

Low trace

This clip takes off a little more hair than the neck and belly clip, but is still a common choice for a pony living both in and out.

High trace

This clip basically follows the same design as the low trace clip, only more hair is removed. It is therefore less suitable for ponies living out.

Chaser

This type of clip leaves most of the body and all of the hindquarters unclipped, but takes off more neck hair. Again, it is suitable for ponies.

Above left: Neck and belly clip.

Above right: Trace clip.

Left: Chaser clip

Blanket

The blanket clip takes off all the neck hair and the head can be completely clipped. This clip is more suitable for the pony that is working harder. Leaving the hair on his back should help prevent him becoming too fresh. It is a useful clip for hunting, as often the pony can be standing around in the cold and wet weather.

Above: Blanket clip.

Below: Hunter clip.

Hunter

This clip is designed for horses and ponies that are working hard. The hair is left on the saddle area and legs, to offer some protection. Removing the hair from the hindquarters will often result in the pony being much fresher when ridden. The hunter clip should therefore be avoided unless the pony is doing a suitable amount of work and being ridden by a competent child. During the summer months, removing all the coat does not usually have the same effect, so could be an option for a pony with a heavy coat.

Full clip.

Full

With this type of clip, all the coat is removed. It is suitable for horses and ponies in harder work.

How to clip

Clipping is something that you should only attempt on your own if you have had previous experience. If not, you are at risk of putting both yourself and your pony in a dangerous situation that may cause an accident. When possible, you should be present when he is being clipped, enabling you to watch, learn and assist when necessary.

There are many freelance grooms who will offer a clipping service. They will usually come to your yard equipped with clippers and everything they need. This is a sensible option if you only have one pony who needs clipping twice a year, as clippers are expensive to buy and maintain.

Preparation

When organising for your pony to be clipped, it is important to ask the person clipping how they would like the pony and clipping area to be prepared.

You will need a suitable indoor area to clip. Some larger yards have a 'clipping box' which will be well equipped for the job. If this is not the case, then you may have to adapt your own stable. The bedding should be put up to the sides. A small amount can be left down if there are no rubber mats to help prevent slipping if the pony gets upset. It is essential to have good lighting. Clipping in the morning is advisable to reduce the risk of running out of daylight. There will need to be a power point close by and sufficient extension cables. Remove all feed and water buckets. A haynet may be provided to help relax the pony. Beware of clipping in an area with a low ceiling and hanging light fixtures.

The pony's coat must be dry and as clean as possible. The clippers will not go through the coat if it is wet or covered in mud. They will also struggle if it is very greasy. It is likely that you will have asked, when buying the pony, if he is good to clip. If possible, let the pony stand close to another one being clipped to note his reaction. This will give you some idea if he is going to be happy with the procedure. It can waste time and money if you book someone to clip your pony and then discover they cannot get near him. Knowing this beforehand will enable you to arrange for the vet to be present to sedate the pony so the job can be done.

It is likely that the person clipping may require your assistance at some stage. It is helpful, even with the quietest pony, to have someone to assist when clipping the head or to pull the legs forward in order to clip under the elbows.

Watching will also give you an opportunity to see how it is done for the future. If the pony is tricky to do but not to the extent that sedation is necessary, it is important that all involved are quiet and patient with him. Getting angry will make him more upset and he is likely to become more difficult to deal with. Try to assess what he does not like.

The following are likely reasons for his discomfort.

- First time being clipped — the pony is unfamiliar with the sound and the feel of the machine.

- Previous bad experience has led to loss of trust in the procedure — the pony may have been nicked by the blades, causing him to associate clipping with pain. He may have been handled badly or burned by hot blades. This often happens when there is lack of time and the job is rushed.

- The pony may be sensitive or ticklish and find it very difficult to tolerate the vibrating blades on his skin.

- The coat is dirty and the blades are pulling at the hair.

If you can assess the reason he is unhappy, it may be possible to make steps towards building his confidence before he is due to be clipped. If he simply does not like the noise, when possible, allow him to stand close to others that are being clipped. If a set of clippers is available, you can stand outside the stable with them running while someone stands inside to reassure him it is okay. Eventually, if he relaxes with this, the clippers can be brought closer until he is happy to have them running next to him. If the pony has lost confidence due to a previous bad experience, only time, patience, good handling and an experienced person to clip will restore this.

A pony that is ticklish or sensitive may never change and this is when it is necessary to sedate. In all cases, it is essential that safety comes first and having to call the vet for assistance is a much better option than someone getting hurt. It is also important to note that even a sedated pony may react at some point during the procedure. This can often catch people out as the pony will have his head on the floor, looking half asleep, and suddenly kick out with a hind leg. If the handler and person clipping are not prepared for this it can result in a nasty injury or a set of broken clippers.

Clockwise: A pony being clipped.

The legs being clipped.

Small clippers being used on the face.

Assistance is required for tricky areas.

Care after clipping

Once the pony has been clipped, he will feel quite itchy. Bathing is the best way to deal with this but is not always practical in the middle of winter unless you are equipped with hot water and heat lamps to dry him off. A useful alternative is to apply hot cloths. A bucket of very hot water with a splash of Dettol, antiseptic wash or baby oil is needed, along with a cloth and rubber gloves. The cloth is soaked and then thoroughly squeezed out, it is then immediately used to scrub the coat. This should only be done to the areas that have been clipped. This is effective in removing loose hairs and thoroughly cleaning the coat. It can be carried

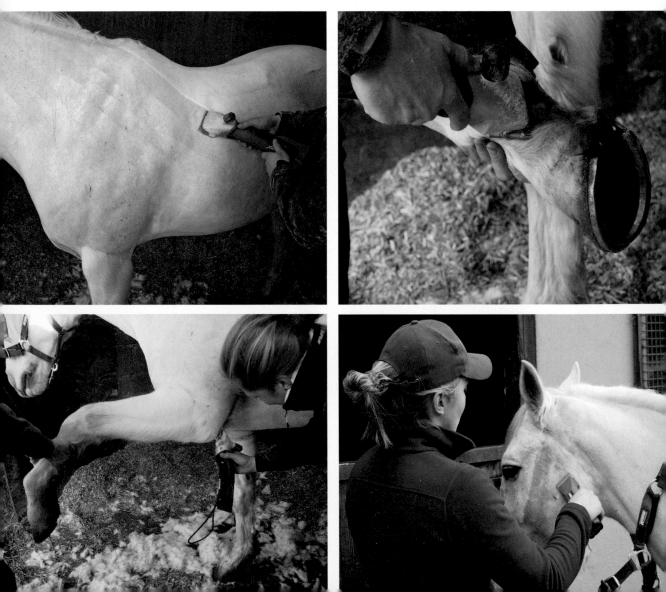

out at any point on a clipped or summer coat as an alternative method of grooming.

The pony will require additional or thicker rugs depending on the type of clip and whether he is stabled or living out. Neck covers are useful when more hair has been removed. Very thick rugs can let in draughts and may not be as effective as they should be. If this is the case, it helps to apply a thinner, more snug-fitting rug underneath. When checking if your pony is warm enough, feel his ears rather than under the rugs as this is a truer indicator. If they are pleasantly warm, he should be warm enough. Over rugging can be as detrimental as under rugging as the pony will become uncomfortable when too hot and have a tendency to roll, which may result in him becoming cast. This is a term used to describe a horse or pony that has rolled and got himself stuck against a wall, usually in a stable. They can often panic and become injured. To avoid this, always check the ear temperature and rug up accordingly.

Extra rugs are required for clipped-out ponies.

Turnout

Trimming

Trimming involves shortening and tidying the mane, tail and hair on the face and the lower legs. It is carried out more frequently on horses and ponies that are being prepared for competition than on those that are kept for pleasure.

Mane pulling and tidying

The mane can be pulled rather than cut. This will thin it as well as shorten it, and give a more natural look. Native breeds should not have their manes pulled, especially if they are going to participate in showing classes. If the pony is living out, a longer, thicker mane will offer warmth and protection from the rain. Not all ponies will readily accept

Native breeds.

the procedure and may need restraining, while others are more resilient. If the pony does not tolerate having his mane pulled there are other methods that can be used.

You will require a small mane comb or 'pulling comb' and latex gloves can be worn to offer protection and help grip the hair. The mane will come out much more easily when the pony is warm. Therefore, the best time to do this is immediately after work or on a warm day; avoid a cold winter's day when the pony has not had any exercise. If you know the pony is happy with the procedure, he can be tied up. If in doubt, have an experienced person hold him. Before you start, decide what length you want the mane to be as it is very easy to get carried away and end up with it too short. If the mane is to be plaited, ensure it is left at a suitable length to do this.

Below: Select a small section of mane.

Bottom: Wrap the hair around the comb.

Start by taking a small section of mane from the centre of the neck, this tends to be the least sensitive area and you will find the mane to be much thicker here. Backcomb the hair towards the crest until a very small amount is left in your hand. This can sometimes be pulled out by giving a sharp, downward tug. If this does not work, wrap the mane tightly around the comb and pull firmly. Comb the mane down and repeat the process, moving up and down the neck. If the pony starts to object, it is wise to leave it for a day or two and go back to it. Hopefully, this way he will learn not to resent the procedure. If the mane has been allowed to get very long and thick, pulling may not be the best method.

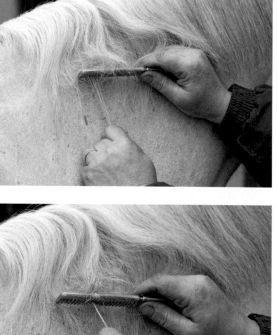

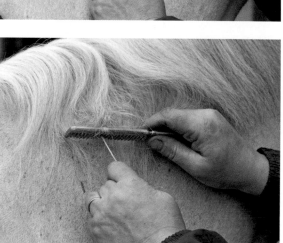

A thinning comb can be used as an alternative to pulling. This cuts the mane rather than pulling it out from the roots. It is less painful for the more sensitive pony. The disadvantage is that it does not thin the mane as much, which then makes plaiting more difficult. There are several types available to buy and all are very user friendly.

Below: A cut mane.

Below right: Scissoring the mane.

Bottom: Cutting the mane.

Cutting/scissoring

The mane can be shortened and tidied by using a large pair of conventional scissors. Again, the mane will not be thinned with this method. Cutting the hair leaves the mane looking very straight and unnatural. Scissoring ensures a more natural look as the hair is cut in an upward direction rather that across.

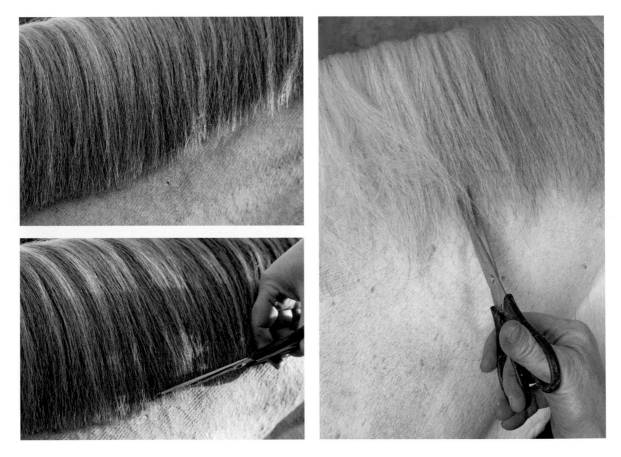

The forelock and bridle path

The forelock can be shortened using any of the above methods. Care should be taken when doing so as it is easy for the pony to bash you in thc face if you stand directly in front of him. A bridle path can be cut to allow the bridle and headcollar to sit comfortably behind the ears without the mane being tangled up in it, which can cause the pony discomfort and consequently make him difficult to bridle. One to two inches of mane is trimmed directly behind the ears using scissors or small clippers. This should not be carried out on native breeds destined for the show ring.

Hogging

Hogging is the term used when the mane is completely removed using the clippers. This is often done on cobs or small, stocky ponies. Polo ponies are also hogged to prevent the mallet getting caught up in the manc. A hogged mane leaves the pony with very little protection on his neck and he may require a neck cover in the winter. The mane also offers a child extra security when riding, as it is quite easy to grab hold of to maintain balance.

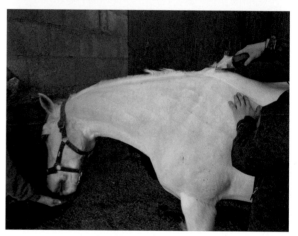

Top: Bridle path.

Above: Hogging the mane.

The mane should be hogged using a good set of clippers with sharp blades. Start at the withers and work up towards the ears. It is essential that the mane is dry and clean before doing so.

Tail pulling and tidying

A pulled tail is more frequently seen on competition horses and hunters, rather than ponies. It is a procedure that should only be attempted by an experienced person as there is a high risk of being kicked or making the tail very sore. The best time to pull the tail is when the pony is warm after working. Hair is removed from the underside of the dock to give the tail a thin, smart, streamlined look. It is not usually necessary

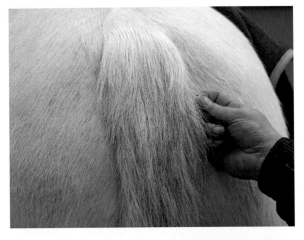

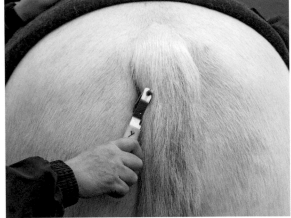

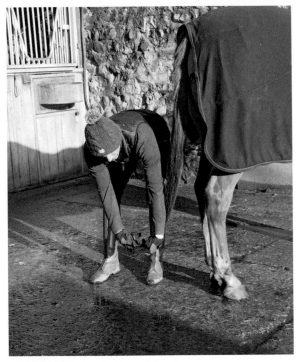

to use the comb unless the hair is very long. A very small amount of hair can be taken between the fingers and a sharp, downwards tug should be sufficient to remove it. The procedure is repeated on both sides of the dock.

Avoid removing too much hair at once as the tail will quickly become sore. Always stand to the side of the pony, never directly behind him. It is usually very clear if he is happy with the procedure and will allow you to carry on. The thinning comb can be used as an alternative method which is often preferred. Native breeds should not have their tails pulled.

Top left: Pulling the tail.

Top right: Using the thinning comb.

Above: Cutting the tail.

At some point, all tails will require trimming at the bottom to shorten the length. Native breeds tend to keep the tail longer and are often trimmed but left with a more natural look. Other tails are usually cut half way between the hock and fetlock. It is advisable to go on the shorter side during the winter to avoid the tail becoming wet and muddy, especially if the pony is living out or hunting. The tail should be clean and tangle free. A large, sharp pair of scissors is then used to cut a neat straight line.

Trimming the legs

Most ponies will grow more hair down the back of their lower legs. These are known as 'feathers'. Cob types and native breeds usually have much more feathers than finer types, and those that are showing must keep their feathers on.

Although there will be less in the summer, feathers do grow all year round. There are several reasons why it may be advantageous to trim the feathers. The legs are easier to clean, will dry much quicker and injuries or skin problems are easier to identify and treat. It also smartens up the pony's appearance. If the pony is living out in winter time, the feathers will offer some protection to the lower legs and heels, as the rain will run off the hair. However, it is still important to check regularly for skin infections and injuries.

Below left: Trimming with comb and scissors.

The feathers can be trimmed using scissors or clippers. If the pony will tolerate the clippers, this is a much quicker and easier method.

Below: Trimming with clippers.

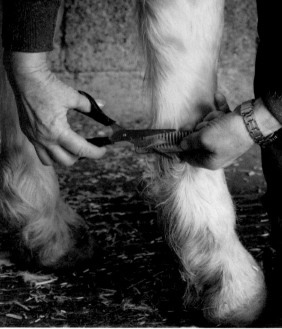

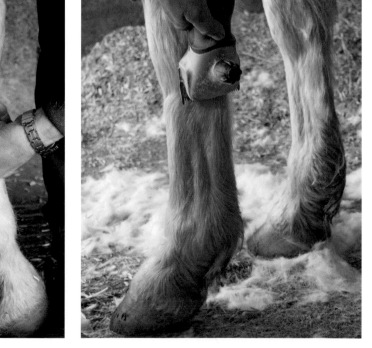

It should be done by an experienced person, as a sudden movement could cause the clippers to cut into the leg. Small, cordless hand clippers are a much safer option. To avoid the clip being too close and not blending in, a grader can be used on the blade. If this is not an option, clip in the direction of the hair, rather than against it. The traditional way of trimming the feathers is by using a comb and scissors. Using scissors alone will create steps in the hair and will look unnatural, cutting besides the teeth of the comb will prevent this.

Trimming the face

Like the legs, the appearance of the pony's head can be improved by trimming the long guard hairs with hand clippers or a comb and scissors. To prevent injury, this should only be done by an experienced person. Again, native breeds intended for showing should not have their faces trimmed.

Plaiting

When going to a competition or Pony Club, it may be necessary to plait your pony's mane and tail. The procedure will take practice and patience, something girls often enjoy. You will need to invest in a plaiting kit.

Plaiting the mane

The mane should be pulled to a suitable length. Wash it a few days before as a very clean mane can be slippery and difficult to hold. A small amount of grease will give a better grip and help the plait to stay in. Brush the mane over to the right-hand side of the neck and lay by using a damp water brush. Use the mane comb to divide a section of hair, each plait should be of similar size and spacing. Use a rubber band on the comb to act as a guide. It is normal to start at the top of the neck and work towards the withers; however, if the pony is head shy, it is advisable to work the other way. Plait

Plaiting kit

- **Large comb**
- **Scissors**
- **Needles**
- **Thread**
- **Plaiting bands**
- **Clip to separate the hair**
- **Water brush**
- **Plaiting spray**
- **Box or bag to hold the kit**
- **Crate or box to stand on.**

the section of hair as tightly as possible, and secure it at the end using a rubber band. Then roll or fold the plait into the neck and apply a second band to secure.

Another option is to secure the plaits using needle and thread. This is more time consuming but looks neater and more suitable for the show

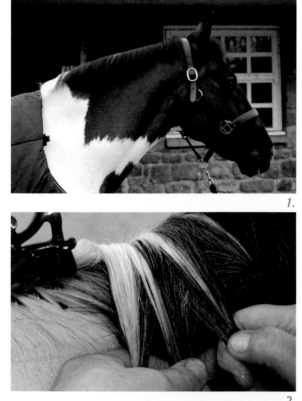

1. *Suitable length for plaiting.*

2. *Divide the mane into three sections.*

3. *Plait the hair.*

4. *Plait being secured with a thread.*

5. *Two neat plaits.*

1.

2.

3.

4.

5.

ring. The forelock can be plaited in the same way or done as a French plait, which looks much smarter.

Plaiting the tail

If your pony's tail is not pulled, it can be plaited but this takes practice. The tail should be clean and brushed out, but not contain products as this will make it very slippery. A French plait is put in the tail, starting as high up as possible. Take a piece of hair from each side and cross the right side over the left, keeping it tight. Take another piece from the left and cross over to give three pieces. Continue taking a piece from alternate sides and crossing them over until you are three quarters of the way down the dock. Try to keep the sections equal size and the tail plait central. The hair is then plaited to the bottom and secured with a rubber band or thread. It is advisable to apply a tail bandage as the pony may try to rub the plait out. All plaits should be taken out immediately on returning home after the competition to avoid the risk of the pony rubbing his mane and tail.

A plaited tail.

15
Transport

If your child joins Pony Club or shows an interest in competing, it is more than likely that you will require some form of transport for the pony. This chapter offers advice on the available options.

Acquiring a horsebox or trailer

Buying

The best option would be to purchase a trailer or small horsebox. A trailer is more common but does require you to have a suitable towing vehicle. You will also need a trailer licence, unless you passed your car driving test before 1 January 1997. A non-heavy goods vehicle (non-HGV), weighing 3.5 to 7.5 tonnes, will also require a specific licence. There are some small horseboxes under 3.5 tonnes that can be driven on a car licence.

Below left:
Horsebox.

Below right:
Checking the tyres.

Having your own transport gives you much more flexibility and means you are not reliant on others. It is not necessary to spend a fortune on a new trailer or horsebox as there are many used ones on the market.

When buying, it is essential to have an experienced person check the vehicle over, not only to see that it is roadworthy but also to check the condition and soundness of the body. A thorough clean and coat of paint can often disguise deterioration in materials, especially wood. Failure to recognise this can lead to a serious accident or injury to the pony, for example a rotten floor not being identified and the pony's foot going through it during transportation.

Hiring

If you are not intending to use a trailer or horsebox very often, then hiring is a sensible option and not too expensive. Companies offer various options on size and type of vehicle. You will pay insurance which will cover you if damage is incurred.

Borrowing

Borrowing a horsebox or trailer from a friend is often risky. Unfortunately, damage is done very easily when transporting. This can be anything from a kick mark to something more serious. It is essential to thoroughly check the vehicle over, inside and out, and it is worth taking a photo of any existing damage. This can be pointed out to the owner before you take it away. Make sure you check the details of the vehicle's insurance policy and that you are actually covered to drive it. If borrowing a trailer, remember to use a temporary number plate to match your car. After use, thoroughly clean out and check over for any damage.

Sharing

Sharing transport can work very well if both parties are intending to leave at the same time and return at a similar time. If not, it can sometimes end up being a very long day. Another problem that can occur is that the ponies may not enjoy travelling together. This should not cause any harm if the partitions are sturdy and the ponies cannot get to one another. Mares tend to be more sensitive when in close contact with others. Conversely, the ponies may become too attached to one another and not take kindly to being separated on arrival. This can present a problem if competing at different times. If a pony is not happy being left alone in a trailer or horsebox he may throw himself around or try to jump out, causing serious injury to himself. If this is the case, the pony should be unloaded at the same time as his friend, and held rather than trying to restrain him by tying up. Even then, he may cause distraction by calling to the other pony, if the other pony then responds it may result in him being disobedient and difficult to ride. If this is the case, it is advisable to look into another option for travelling next time.

Travel equipment

To travel your pony safely and avoid injury, it is advisable for him to wear protective clothing.

Tail bandage

A pony will often rub his tail while travelling and a bandage can help prevent damage to the hair. It is essential that this is applied with the correct amount of tension and not left on for longer than necessary. If you are concerned that the pony may dirty his tail, it is wise to plait it down to the bottom and apply a second bandage to cover the entire tail. For longer journeys, a tail guard is a more suitable option as this cannot be applied too tightly and is therefore more comfortable.

Travel boots

Travelling in the back of a horsebox or trailer is extremely unbalancing and often ponies will move about and are at risk of banging or treading on themselves. Boots can be applied to reduce the risk of injury. They are designed to cover the foreleg from above the knee to the ground and hind leg from above the hock. They should fit quite snugly to ensure they don't slip, but not so tight that they will create problems. Traditionally, bandages and fibregee were used. This method is time consuming and, again, problems can occur if the bandages are put on too tight or left on for long periods of time.

Travel rugs

A travel rug may need to be worn in colder weather or to keep the pony clean when going to a competition. A pony will often get hot when travelling and can be prone to sweating, even on colder days. This is more likely to happen to a pony who is nervous about travelling. It can also happen when a number of horses and ponies are travelling together, especially if the horsebox is not well ventilated. The best type of rug to use is a cooler, as this will absorb sweat and stay dry on the inside, preventing the pony getting chilly as he cools down.

Whilst travelling, it is essential that the horsebox or trailer is well ventilated. Lack of fresh air can lead to respiratory problems, especially

A pony suitably dressed for travelling.

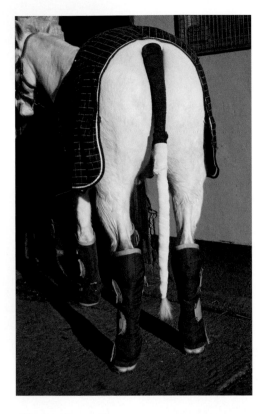

Above: Two tail bandages used to keep the tail clean.

Right: Haynet tied too low.

when a number of horses are sharing and on longer journeys. In cold weather, do not be tempted to reduce the ventilation to keep the pony warmer, additional rugs should be worn instead.

Additional equipment

There are additional items that are necessary to have when travelling. It is useful if you have a separate set from those you use in the stable. This enables you to prepare and pack the day before the competition, which is helpful when you have an early start.

If your horsebox does not have a water tank, you will need water containers to carry fresh water for drinking and washing down. Water is often not available at a competition. Never allow your pony to drink from water troughs in fields as there may be a risk of disease.

It is useful to have two water buckets. At the competition, one can be filled for drinking and the other for washing off. A sponge and sweat scraper will also be needed for this.

The pony should travel with a haynet, this can help relax him during the journey. Avoid using very large haynets for travelling as they can take up a lot of the pony's space and end up hanging very low as they empty, creating a risk that the pony might get his foot stuck in it.

When travelling, it is advisable to carry an equine first aid kit. This can be your one from the yard or, if possible, a separate one that stays with the trailer or horsebox. It should contain the essentials for treating minor wounds and injuries.

Loading

Not all ponies are good travellers and some get very stressed. If you have ever stood with a horse in a moving horsebox or trailer you will understand why. It is quite an unbalancing experience, some find this easier to cope with than others. If you do notice your pony is struggling, observe him to see how he wants to position himself. Some prefer to spread their hind legs wide and therefore need a bigger space, while others prefer to lean against the partition and are better with a smaller space.

If your pony doesn't like travelling, he may not be easy to load. It is very common to see people at competitions struggling to get their ponies back on the trailer or horsebox. This can be very frustrating at the end of a long day. It can also cause you to be late arriving at events or lessons.

Time should be taken to build up the pony's confidence and trust. This needs to be supervised by an experienced person and not attempted when you may run out of time. To begin with, practise loading and unloading without actually travelling anywhere. Position the trailer or horsebox in a quiet area where the pony will not be distracted. A more enclosed space may help if there are fewer escape areas. Make the ramp as flat as possible. Open partitions wide and make the area light. The pony should wear his travel boots to protect his legs and a bridle or pressure headcollar. Your instructor can advise you on what equipment is necessary.

It can help to have another quiet pony already loaded, this will often encourage the pony as his natural instinct is to follow. Allow the pony to take his time and do not become angry if he does not load immediately. The pony has to learn to trust the handler if he is going to develop the confidence to follow them into the horsebox. A second person may assist to keep the pony straight, but having too many people around can make him distressed and confusing for him. A nervous pony can often kick and many accidents occur when a person stands directly behind and tries to chase the pony in. Care must be taken, even with the most trustworthy animal. Children should not be encouraged to help and should stand well away from the area.

Once the pony is in, the helper can assist to close the partitions, as the pony may want to come out immediately. The pony should only be tied to a secure tie ring that is fitted with a thin piece of bale string or a quick-release link. Do not be tempted to tie up to any other fittings. Never tie up the pony before the partitions are closed. Give him lots of praise and allow him to stand for a while. Offering a small feed or haynet will often help reassure him and he will consider the ordeal a more positive experience. Repeat this several times until he is happily loading without resistance.

Right: Patience is required when loading.

Below: Lead the pony calmly up the centre of the ramp.

Below right: An assistant closes the partition.

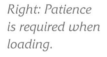

Once this is accomplished, take the pony for a short drive. At this stage. it is better for him not to associate travelling with an equally stressful or exciting experience at the other end. If this is done on a regular basis, hopefully he will become easier. It may need to be done between competitions if he has had a setback. Always remember to allow plenty of time for loading when going to a competition or lesson. It is much better to arrive early if all has gone to plan than arrive late with a pony that is already stressed and, more than likely, an upset child.

When driving horses and ponies, care must be taken when braking and going round turns. Drive at a slower speed than normal, slow down and accelerate gradually. This will give your pony a much smoother ride and hopefully he will not be too worried about travelling. If at any point during the journey you hear or feel a lot of movement coming from the horse area, it is essential to pull over immediately and check what is happening. If the pony has got into difficulty, failing to help him may end up in a serious injury.

Unloading

On arrival at the competition or event, the pony should be checked immediately to ensure he has had a trouble-free journey. Take time to check that he does not feel too warm and that his rug and boots are in place. The haynet may need tying up and he can also be offered a drink. If he has travelled a long distance, it is advisable to unload him to give his legs a stretch and let him graze for a short time. You may notice white discharge from one or both nostrils when the pony puts his head down. This occurs due to the fact that he has been travelling, tied up, with his head quite high, eating hay. If allowed to graze he can clear his airway and this should not be a problem when ridden.

When unloading, it may be necessary to have assistance to open partitions. Some trailers require the pony to reverse out. If this is the case, a helper can assist in guiding him down the ramp. Some ponies will be keen to leave the horsebox and can become impatient. In this instance, an adult must handle him as he will be too strong for a child. The pony should be untied before opening the partition, otherwise he may try to leave and panic when he feels the restraint. Once the pony is untied and the partitions are opened as wide as possible, the pony should be encouraged to unload patiently. If he is a handful, a bridle should be worn. When unloading on the yard, choose a safe place, preferably with a non-slip surface, especially if he is keen to be home.

16
Selling the pony

For most people, the time will come when you will have to sell your pony. This can often be quite a distressing time for all as he may have become a much-loved member of the family. In other cases, it may simply be that he has not turned out to be the right pony and the attachment to him does not exist. Either way, it should be your intention to find him a new, suitable home.

Child has outgrown their pony.

224

Reasons for selling

- Outgrown

- More capable pony required

- Child lost interest

- Child lost confidence

- Pony not suitable

- Financial reasons

- Moving house to unsuitable location.

Loaning

In some cases, it may be that sending your pony out on loan is a more desirable option as you have a younger child that is not yet big enough to take him on. You may feel so attached that you do not want to sell him as there is a risk of losing track of where he ends up and what sort of home he gets. Sending the pony out on loan means you do not have the financial burden of caring for him, but does require you to have the funds to be able to replace him if your child is still interested and wants another pony.

If you have a good pony, finding a loan home will not prove a problem. Once you put the word out that he is available, it is likely you will be inundated with enquiries. It is then up to you to find the most suitable home and rider for him. Being spoiled for choice puts you in a fortunate position, and means you can 'vet' the family. Once they have tried the pony and you are happy with how he is ridden, you can then visit the new home to check it is a suitable place for him to live, and that he is going to be well looked after.

It is essential, as discussed earlier, that a loan contract is agreed between both parties and signed. This can sometimes be overlooked or considered unnecessary if the pony is being 'borrowed' by a friend.

This is a big mistake as when things go wrong it can cause numerous problems, and perhaps loss of a friendship. One of the most important things to consider is the time scale of the agreement, especially if you are wanting him back for a second child. This can prove a tricky situation if your child is ready before the loan home wants to give him up. The other important consideration is what happens if, for some reason, the pony can no longer be ridden due to ill health or injury but the loan agreement still has six months left. Who will cover the financial side? When loaning out your pony, it is inevitable that at some stage he will need to retire and come back to you. Are you in a position to take him back if you have another pony at home?

Advertising

If your pony has been successful with your child, and they have participated in competitions and Pony Club activities, it is highly likely that you will have been approached by people asking you to contact them when the time comes to sell. Many good ponies have a list of future homes to go to. This is an ideal situation as it saves time advertising and dealing with time wasters or unsuitable buyers. It also gives you peace of mind knowing where the pony is going and that he will hopefully be well looked after.

If this is not the case, then start to put the word out that your pony will be coming up for sale through Pony Club and instructors. It is often a good idea to give some notice as to when that may be, as it gives a potential buyer time to think about selling their present pony if this needs to be done first.

The time of year can often influence the amount of interest you get. Fewer people will be looking to buy during the winter months. Advertising the pony prior to school holidays, such as Easter and summer, will allow more opportunities for children to try the pony.

Pony Club may have a website that offers a 'For Sale' section that your pony can be advertised on. This is often free of charge. If this does

Left: An example of a suitable photograph for advertising.

Below: Although a nice photograph, this does not show the pony from a good angle.

not raise interest, then it may be necessary to place an advert on a website or in a magazine. This can be quite expensive and often involves speaking to time wasters.

When using a website, your pony will be one of hundreds. Therefore, you need to ensure that your advert is eye catching, otherwise it may easily be overlooked. Your advert can usually include photos, and sometimes also links to videos. Ensure that the main photo you use is one that shows the pony at his best. This can be in hand, without tack, or being ridden. Whichever you decide on, it should show him off fully and not just his head. Ensure he has his ears pricked and looks a 'happy' pony. This photo will be the first thing a potential buyer looks at, and if it is not flattering they are likely

CHILD'S DREAM PONY

14hh, 14-year-old, Connemara, grey gelding

Regrettably, the time has come for us to sell our much-loved pony.

William has been with us for five years, giving both my children much pleasure and success competing, hunting and participating in all Pony Club activities. He is forward thinking but polite and only ever ridden in a snaffle. He goes nicely on the flat and loves to jump. He is not spooky and jumps coloured fences and cross country, including ditches and water. Hacks alone and in company.

William is a pleasure to look after and adores attention from the children. He is good to catch, shoe, box, clip and has never shown any vices. He has never been lame and is open to vetting. Fully vaccinated and up to date with worming and the dentist.

Excellent facilities available to try. William still has much to offer and we are looking for a five-star home.

£5500 including bridle and selection of rugs.

More photos and video available.

to quickly move onto the next. If the website allows you to use more than one photo, choose a variety showing the pony doing different activities.

The wording in your advert should have an eye-catching title that is going to encourage people to read on. It should then have an accurate description of the pony, including height, type, age and gender. Then describe in more detail what activities the pony has done, his temperament both ridden and in the stable, any vices, the reason for sale, facilities available for trying and, finally, the price.

Dealing with buyers

Be prepared to have accurate information about your pony readily available to you when buyers respond to your advert. If you are working and cannot take a call until the evening, it is wise to state this in the advert; buyers can be put off if they try to get hold of you unsuccessfully on numerous occasions. Once you have given them the information they require about the pony, it is wise to ask them questions to ascertain if their child is suitable. This can save a lot of time wasting on both sides.

If you are happy with someone on the basis of the above information, you can arrange a suitable time for them to try the pony. This should be at a time when the arena will be quiet. Don't try to tire the pony out before they come, in the hope that he will not misbehave. It is better for both parties that the pony is tried as he is and it is clear whether or not the potential buyer is capable of riding him.

QUESTIONS TO ASK
POTENTIAL BUYERS

◊ How old is their child and are they average size for their age?
◊ How long have they ridden?
◊ What level are they riding at?
◊ What type of pony have they ridden?
◊ Is this their first pony or have they owned prior to this?
◊ Where do they intend to keep the pony?
◊ Do they have regular lessons and attend Pony Club?

You will usually get an idea, fairly quickly, if you warm to the people and think they will be suitable. Take note of how confident they are around the pony; do they look as if they have had previous experience or more like a duck out of water? If it is the latter, do not be immediately put off as everyone has to start somewhere. They should, however, be accompanied by an instructor and not be planning on taking the pony home and caring for it without advice.

Ensure you ask all the right questions.

This will be a very difficult time for you and your child, as the thought of parting with your much-loved pony will be tough. It is important that this does not influence the way your child rides the pony when showing him to the potential buyers. If this proves too difficult, then it may be necessary to explain this to the buyers and have a friend help out. Avoid this, if possible, as it may raise suspicion if your child does not ride their pony.

Allow the child plenty of time to try the pony. If, however, at any point you feel they are out of their depth or unsuitable, it is wise to step in. The buyer may also appreciate your help and advice when getting to know the pony. This works very well if it is done from child to child.

If all goes well, it is likely they will want to try him a second time. This should be allowed if you are confident they are suitable and not out of their depth. It is best to do this as soon as possible as you may have others interested in him. Be cautious of offering a trial period, as discussed in Chapter 4. If the potential buyer is known to you then it may be considered.

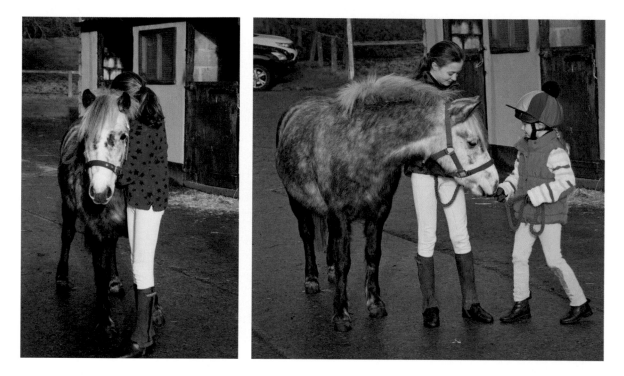

Saying goodbye to the pony

Once a deal has been negotiated and your pony has found a new home, you will need to prepare to say goodbye. This can be tough on all the family, especially if he has been with you for a number of years. For your child, it may feel like the worst day of their lives. Allow them to have some special time together before the day comes. It is likely that your child may feel some guilt towards their pony and will want to spoil him, so have lots of carrots and apples in stock! It is nice to have something of your pony to remember him by. Your child may appreciate keeping his browband as a memento or having a bracelet or necklace made from his tail hair.

Going to see your pony's new home may help all of you come to terms with his departure. It is likely that the new owners will keep in touch with his progress and be happy for you to visit. It is good to give advice when asked but important not to interfere too much, remember you no longer own the pony.

Above left: Give the child time to say goodbye. Saying goodbye can be upsetting.

Above right: The new owner is handed the pony.

The pony leaving with the new owner and dealing with a heartbroken child.

More than anything, moving on to the next pony will help your child come to terms with the sale. Start looking for the next one before your old pony has gone and try to arrange some ponies to view as soon as possible.

17
Learn from *my* mistakes

In this final chapter, I would like to share with you some of my own personal experiences buying, owning and caring for the ponies I had as a child.

I started riding at my local riding school when I was about six years old. My parents were not horsey and had no experience, but were very supportive. I continued for about three years, progressing quite well and developing into a pony-mad child. I remember it was all I ever wanted, and I spent lots of time with friends who owned their own ponies. Of course, this then led to me being desperate to have my own. Coming from a working class family in which both parents worked, we were not wealthy and time was short, this was not an easy decision.

A friend then offered me her pony to loan as she had outgrown him. Eventually, my parents agreed and we took on a 12.2hh, Welsh mountain pony called Tiny Tam. Fortunately, this worked out really well. I say fortunately because we did not have any form of loan agreement with his owners, it was all very casual. He continued to live at the farm where he had been at livery. His owner was also there and assisted me in looking after him. I kept him for about a year, learned a lot and had lots of fun.

Below left: My first pony.

Below right: A friend's pony.

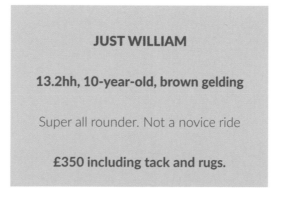

Above: Tiny Tam.

After about a year, I grew too big for him and my parents decided we could look for something bigger to buy. I had not joined Pony Club at this stage and did not have a regular instructor. I think we thought we had learned a lot over the past year and having not had any problems ... what could possibly go wrong?

We came across an advert in a local newspaper.

Not a novice ride! This should have immediately raised alarm bells, but I did not class my eleven-year-old self as a 'novice', as I had been riding for years.

JUST WILLIAM

13.2hh, 10-year-old, brown gelding

Super all rounder. Not a novice ride

£350 including tack and rugs.

My parents and I went to try the pony without an instructor or adviser. The lady who we dealt with told us she was selling him on behalf of a client; in other words, she was a dealer. We did not think to question this. He was a beautiful looking pony and I fell in love immediately. I was put straight up on him, without seeing anyone ride him first. He was wearing a pelham, which is quite a severe bit. Again, we did not think to question this either. I rode him in a tiny grass paddock and jumped some small cross-country jumps. He went very nicely, if not a little strong. I loved him and wanted him. We told the dealer we were interested and would have a think about it. She replied saying that she would need an answer tomorrow as she had other people wanting to see him. I begged and pleaded with my parents and eventually they agreed we would buy him. No more questions were asked, no vetting, just total trust in what we had been told. We collected him a few days later.

We had not had William for more than a week when I went for a hack with my friend. At some point on the ride he got a scare and bolted with me. We went for quite a distance before I managed to stop in a ploughed field. This resulted in a very lame pony. Having had no experience with lameness, we thought we had better call the vet. The vet came the next day, by which time William had developed a very hot, swollen front leg. The vet diagnosed a substantial injury to the suspensory ligament and told us it was apparent that this was not a new injury but one that had been masked very well for a sale. The prognosis was not good but we would try rest and treatment to see if the injury would heal.

Unfortunately, after months of rest, as soon as he started to work again, the injury reoccurred and we were advised not carry on treatment. The only positive thing was that we had insured him for vets' fees and death. Therefore, financially, we could think about replacing him. However, this did not compensate for the heartache it caused as we did have the pony put down. This was a massive learning curve as we just about made every possible mistake I have written about.

The next pony we bought was a 13.2hh, nine-year-old gelding called Conka. Again, we went to try the pony without a professional to guide us. We were told he was for sale as he had proved 'too much' for his current rider. I was very brave as a child and not easily put off! He was not shown to us ridden, as there was not a small enough rider available to ride him. I tried him and fell off three times. I still wanted him, as his jump was amazing.

Again, I managed to persuade my parents to buy him. It was, in theory, a big mistake but in the end it worked out very well. I joined Pony Club and got the help I needed. He was an amazing show jumping pony, I just had to learn how to ride him. It took me about two years before this happened. I kept him for three years and we won numerous competitions towards the end. It is quite typical that a child eventually gets the hang of a pony when it is time to move him on. We could have sold him a hundred times over and made a substantial profit on him. The girl who bought him from us continued to have lots of success.

Having Conka had given me a real taste for show jumping and this is what I wanted to do. It was suggested by someone that we go to a reputable dealer who specialises in show jumping ponies. Again, we went to look on our own. There were lots of ponies to look at, unfortunately all quite expensive as they were good quality. The ponies that had some experience were all out of our budget, so the dealer suggested that we look at a young pony that I could produce. He showed us several five year olds loose jumping. They showed good form and jumped nicely. I particularly liked a 14.2hh, five-year-old, brown gelding. I rode him in the arena and, although he felt green, I coped.

Conka.

237

The dealer persuaded us that, with the right help, I was more than capable of bringing him on and in a few years' time, after competing, we would be able to sell him for a lot of money. Like any good dealer, he knew how to sell and we went ahead and bought him. Even though he was young, he still cost us more than we had hoped to pay.

Having made so many mistakes, you would have thought that we would have learned our lesson. Unfortunately not! This time we faced different problems. Flight was a nice pony to have and not a total disaster. I was now having lessons with a professional show jumping trainer and his jumping did progress nicely. However, we did have two major problems.

Firstly, he had obviously never been ridden on the road and was very nervous in traffic. This was not ideal for me as I had to ride along quite a busy road in order to get to the quieter lanes and bridle paths. His confidence did not improve and, if anything, he became more nervous.

The second problem we had was not realising that five year olds can still have quite a lot of growing to do. Flight was bred in Ireland and, typically, he kept growing until he was six. When we bought him he was already on the large side of 14.2hh, a year later he was 15hh. Affiliated competitions require ponies to be measured and given a height certificate to prove they are the correct height for the classes they are jumping in. The maximum height a pony can be is 14.2hh. I still had two years left

Flight.

LEARN FROM *MY* MISTAKES

in which I was eligible to jump in pony classes and this is what I wanted to do. We would have to sell him. This decision was made easier by the problems with traffic when out hacking.

I was then offered a loan pony by my instructor. Pendle Witch was the last pony I had. She was a 14.1hh, sixteen-year-old, chestnut mare. Witch belonged to my instructor. In her younger years, my instructor and her brother competed Witch at top level, including being part of a silver-medal European show jumping team. Now retired from top level, they wanted her to have an easier life.

Above and left:
Pendle Witch.

Even at the age of sixteen, she had so much to give and gave me an opportunity beyond my wildest dreams. I competed at some big county shows and represented my Pony Club on numerous show jumping teams.

I hope that by reading about my experiences, you have learnt what not to do! I also hope that you can see that sometimes a negative can become a positive if you get the right help and don't give up. If I could change the past, I don't know that I would, as my experience growing up with ponies gave me the determination and ambition to carry on and make it a career. Now the mother of a pony-mad daughter, I can try to avoid making the same mistakes when buying ponies for her.

*Pony-mad
daughter with Sox.*

Glossary

Glossary

- **Basic handling** – Skills required to enable a person to safely carry out daily tasks such as tying up, grooming, leading and turning out a pony.
- **Bombproof** – Describes a pony that is unlikely to react and get upset by objects, noise or activity going on around him.
- **British Horse Society (BHS)** – Britain's largest equestrian charity, www.bhs.org.uk.
- **Camp** – Organised by Pony Club branches, children and their ponies spend a week with friends. They care for their ponies and receive lessons and lectures, along with other fun activities.
- **Concentrates (hard feed)** – Commercial pre-mixed feed or grain.
- **Conformation** – The physical appearance of the pony relating to his skeletal structure and body proportions.
- **Cracked heels** – A bacterial skin infection that causes scabs to form on the heels. When these scabs fall off it can leave painful sores.
- **Crest** – Fatty deposits along the top of the pony's neck.
- **Dealer** – A person who buys and sells horses and ponies.
- **Digital pulse** – Blood flowing through the artery into the hoof. Inflammation in the hoof restricts blood flow resulting in a strong digital pulse.
- **Dock** – The upper part of the tail consisting of muscle and skin covering the coccygeal vertebrae.
- **Farrier** – A specialist in equine hoof care and shoeing.
- **Feathers** – Long hair growing on the lower leg, commonly seen on native breeds.
- **Feed balancer** – A concentrated supplement containing protein, vitamins and minerals.
- **Fetlock** – The joint on the leg situated between the cannon bone and the pastern.
- **Flank** – The area on the pony's body between the ribs and the hip.
- **Foreleg** – The front leg.

- **Forelock** – The section of mane that grows from the poll and falls on the face.
- **Freelance instructor/groom** – A self-employed person who travels to different yards to offer their services.
- **Frog** – Triangular structure found on the inside of the hoof.
- **Good mouth** – Refers to a pony that doesn't fight the bit, become fussy in the mouth or get strong.
- **Growth rings** – Rings found on the hoof wall which can be a result of laminitis.
- **Hack** – To ride outside an enclosed area either on the road or a bridleway.
- **Head shy** – Defensive behaviour displayed by raising the head or moving away when attempting to fit a headcollar or bridle. The pony may also be nervous of having his head stroked or brushed.
- **Hock** – The joint in the hind leg situated between the stifle and fetlock.
- **Lameness** – Abnormal movement or stance, commonly caused by pain.
- **Livery yard** – A yard that provides owners' horses with stabling and/or grazing (and sometimes other services) for a fee.
- **Lungeing** – A form of exercise or training in which the pony is worked on a circle around the handler using a lunge line (long rope).
- **Napping** – Resistance to go forward or perform, usually caused by discomfort.
- **Neck strap** – A leather strap fitted around the pony's neck during riding. The rider should use the neck strap instead of the reins to support their balance when necessary.
- **Numnah** – A pad used under the saddle, usually made from cotton or sheepskin.
- **On trial** – A period of time given to take a pony home to try before buying.
- **Over-stocked** – A field that is too small for the number of livestock grazing.
- **Pony Club** – A voluntary organisation found worldwide. It aims to

educate children in both riding and stable management, giving them the opportunity to work towards tests and competitions.

- **Pony Club tests** – Proficiency tests designed to encourage members to progressively improve their riding and stable management skills.
- **Poo picking** – Removal of droppings from the paddock or arena.
- **Rallies** – Mounted or unmounted tuition for Pony Club members.
- **Riding Club** – A club for amateur riders offering a range of activities, tuition and competitions.
- **Risen clenches** – A clench is the name given to the nail where it emerges through the hoof wall. A risen clench is a sign the pony needs the farrier.
- **Roughage** – Feed containing a lot of crude fibre which is essential in keeping the digestive system healthy.
- **Sales** – An auction selling horses and ponies.
- **Schoolmaster** – An older, experienced pony that has competed and done Pony Club activities.
- **Simple snaffle** – A commonly used mild bit.
- **Skip/skip out** – A skip is a large plastic tub used to collect droppings from the stable. Skipping out is the removal of droppings from the stable.
- **Stabled** – A pony that lives in a stable rather than a field.
- **Stable management** – All aspects of caring for a horse or pony.
- **Starvation paddock** – A small, fenced off area in the field offering very little grass, intended to limit the amount of grazing.
- **Sweat scraper** – Used to remove excess water from the coat after bathing.
- **Tacked up** – A pony that is wearing a saddle and bridle ready to be ridden.
- **Traffic proof** – A pony that is confident and safe to be ridden on a busy road.
- **Twisted shoe** – A shoe that has moved but is still attached to the hoof requiring immediate removal.
- **Weigh tape** – A tape that is used to estimate a pony's weight using body measurements.

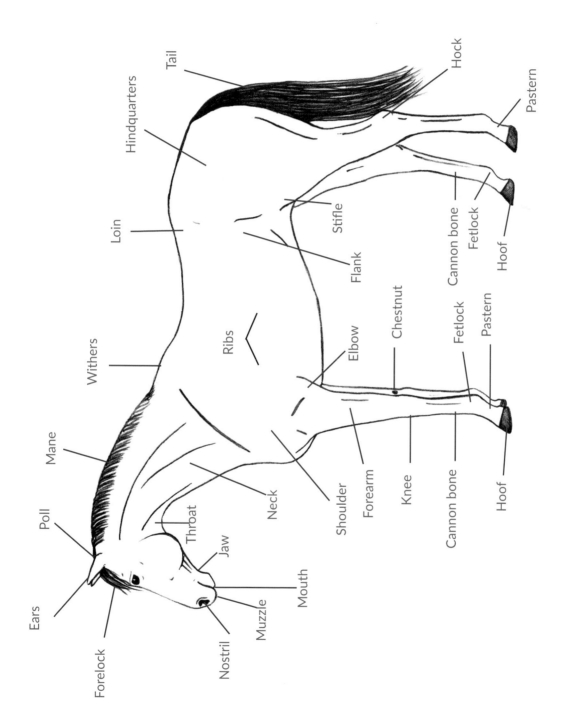

Parts of the horse

245

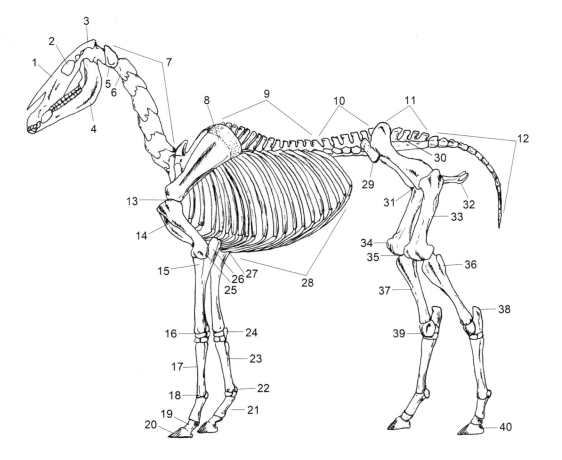

Points of the skeleton

1	Skull / Cranium	15	Radius	29	Tuber Coaxe
2	Orbit	16	Knee Joint	30	Sacrum
3	Occiput	17	Cannon Bone	31	Hip Joint
4	Mandible	18	Fetlock Joint	32	Ischium
5	Atlas	19	Short Pastern	33	Femur
6	Axis	20	Pedal Bone	34	Patella
7	Cervical Vertebrae	21	Long Pastern	35	Stifle Joint
8	Scapula	22	Sesamoids	36	Fibula
9	Thoracic Vertebrae	23	Splint Bone	37	Tibia
10	Lumbar Vertebrae	24	Accessory Carpal	38	Tuber Calcis
11	Sacral Vertebrae	25	Elbow Joint	39	Hock Joint
12	Caudal Vertebrae (Tail)	26	Ulna	40	Navicular Bone
13	Shoulder Joint	27	Sternum		
14	Humerus	28	Ribs		